Fantasy Art Creatures

Drawing Your Favorite Fantasy Creatures

by Jong Mac

Table of Contents

Disclaimer

While all attempts have been made to verify the information provided in this book, the author does assume any responsibility for errors, omissions, or contrary interpretations of the subject matter contained within. The information provided in this book is for educational and entertainment purposes only. The reader is responsible for his or her own actions and the author does not accept any responsibilities for any liabilities or damages, real or perceived, resulting from the use of this information.

The trademarks that are used are without any consent, and the publication of the trademark is without permission or backing by the trademark owner. All trademarks and brands within this book are for clarifying purposes only and are the owned by the owners themselves, not affiliated with this document.

Introduction

For fantasy lovers, part of the great love of their favorite fantasy stories stems from the art. The Orcs of *Lord of the Rings* are infamous, and vampires have always had a place in fantastic literature. Sirens are what lured Odysseus' crew in mythology, and every villain needs a henchman.

Drawing itself can be very rewarding, but drawing fantasy art has unique rewards of its own. Fantasy artists can create comics and illustrate beautifully written worlds, like *Shannara* or *Discworld*. Tabletop games need their villains, or the battles would never work.

Drawing can be a relaxing and fun pastime, whether it be hobby or career. The feeling and sounds of a pencil on paper can be a soothing one, and the motion of drawing itself is very calming. For children, drawing can improve fine motor skills, or skills that involve very precise movements, such as cutting, writing, and playing instruments. These fine motor skills can then improve gross motor skills, like walking, running, and jumping.

Fantasy art can be found all around us, in video games and movies. Children's shows are full of fantastical ideas, and even mobile games have started to create vivid storylines that require only the best fantasy art. Consider *Final Fantasy*, one of the leading games when it comes to fantasy – it features interesting characters, inspiring settings, and fantastic creatures, all of which work to draw you into the plotline and keep you hooked. People fall in love with these characters and begin to care about what happens to them, partly because they look so good.

So, improving your art skill when it comes to fantasy art can be incredibly important to your comic, book or game – it can help sell your product while also giving you an activity full of rich enjoyment.

Creating your own fantasy art is both fun and relaxing. This book is a step-by-step guide to drawing your own fantasy creatures, be they friend or foe. In this book, you'll learn how to draw an Orc, a Dark Pixie Girl, a Siren, a Horned Girl, a Vampire, and a Snake Shifter, all ready to either help your hero or hurt your heroine. Tools you'll need include paper and pencil. You'll want to go for a drawing pencil instead of a mechanical pencil so you can vary the pressure as needed. So sit back, get ready to draw, and enjoy filling your fantasy world with terrifying creatures!

Chapter 1 – Orc

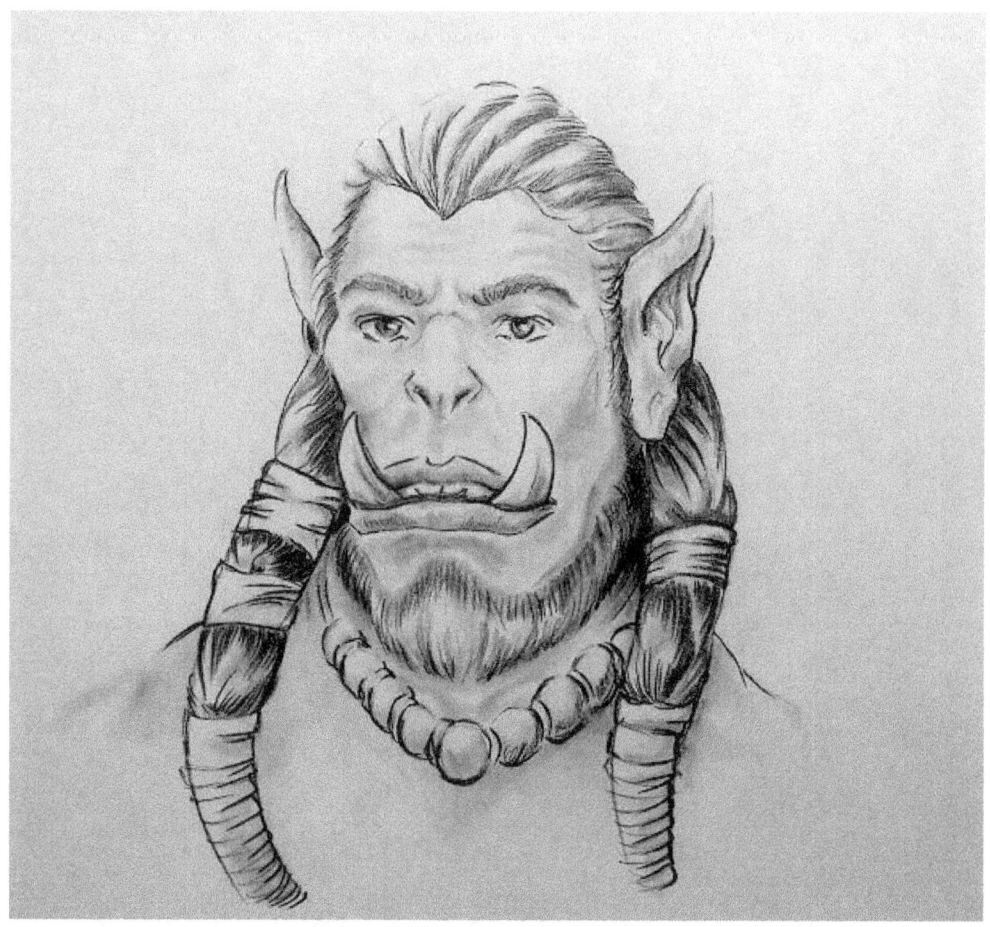

One of the most famous creatures in fantasy games and stories is the Orc. Usually, the Orc is a villain, but can sometimes be a powerful ally. This particular Orc is wise, probably a tribe elder.

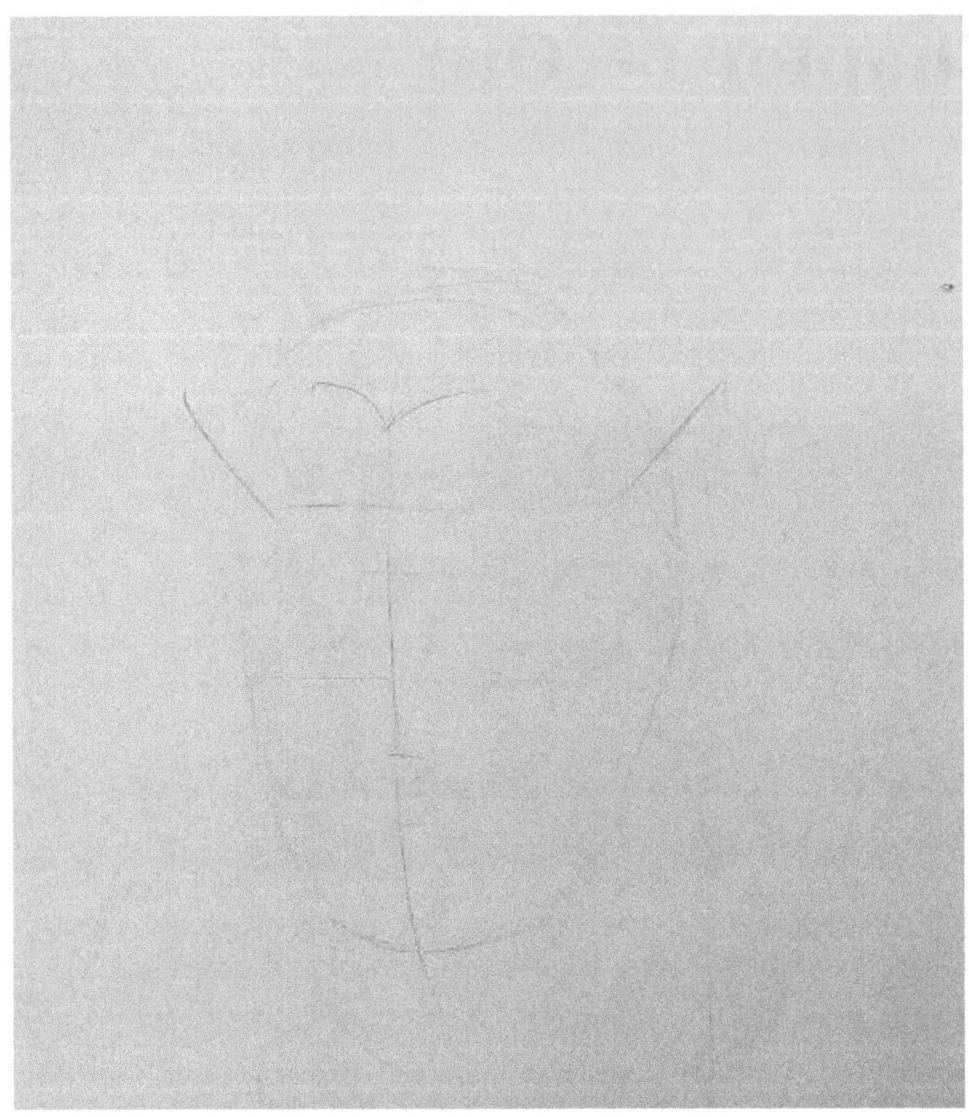

First, start with a basic outline of the face, drawing lines to indicate the hairline, the ears, and where the eyes and nose will go. The line down the middle shows which way the Orc is facing.

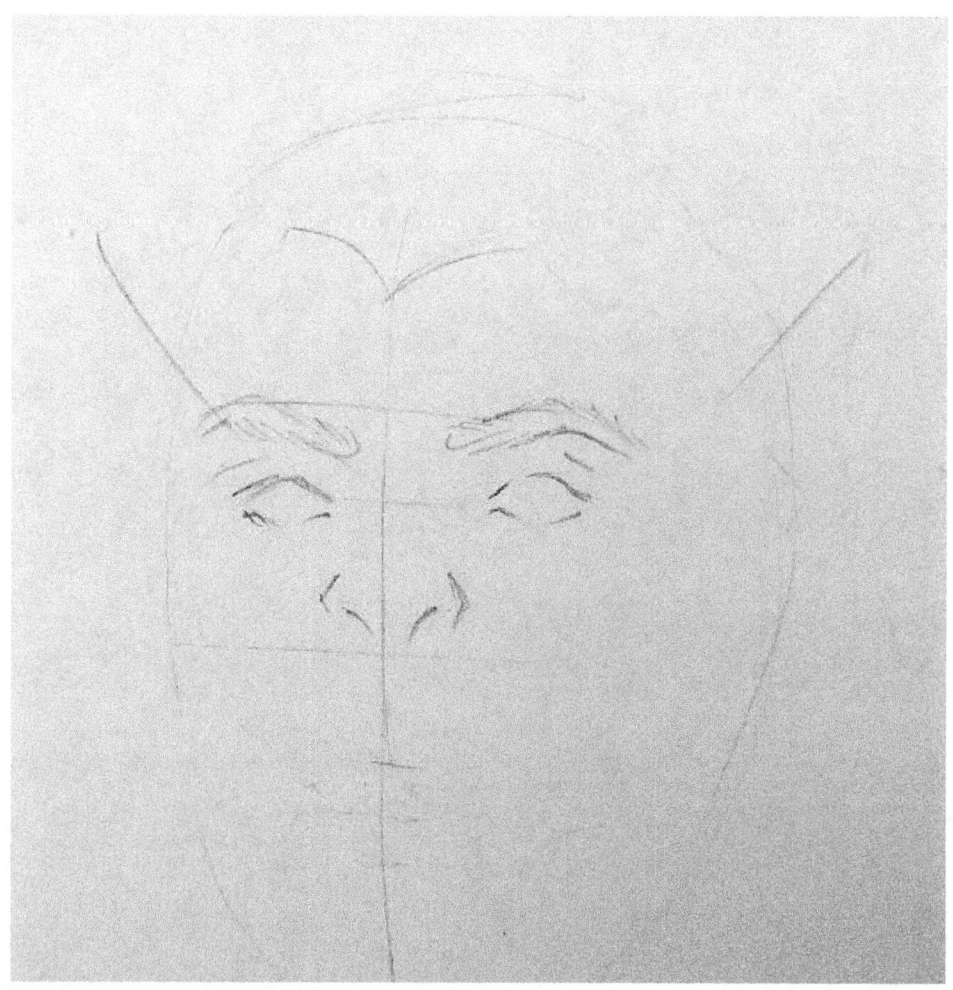

Now do a little detail work. Get the outline of the eyes and the nose in, and start working on the Orc's bushy eyebrows. These will give him a wizened sort of look.

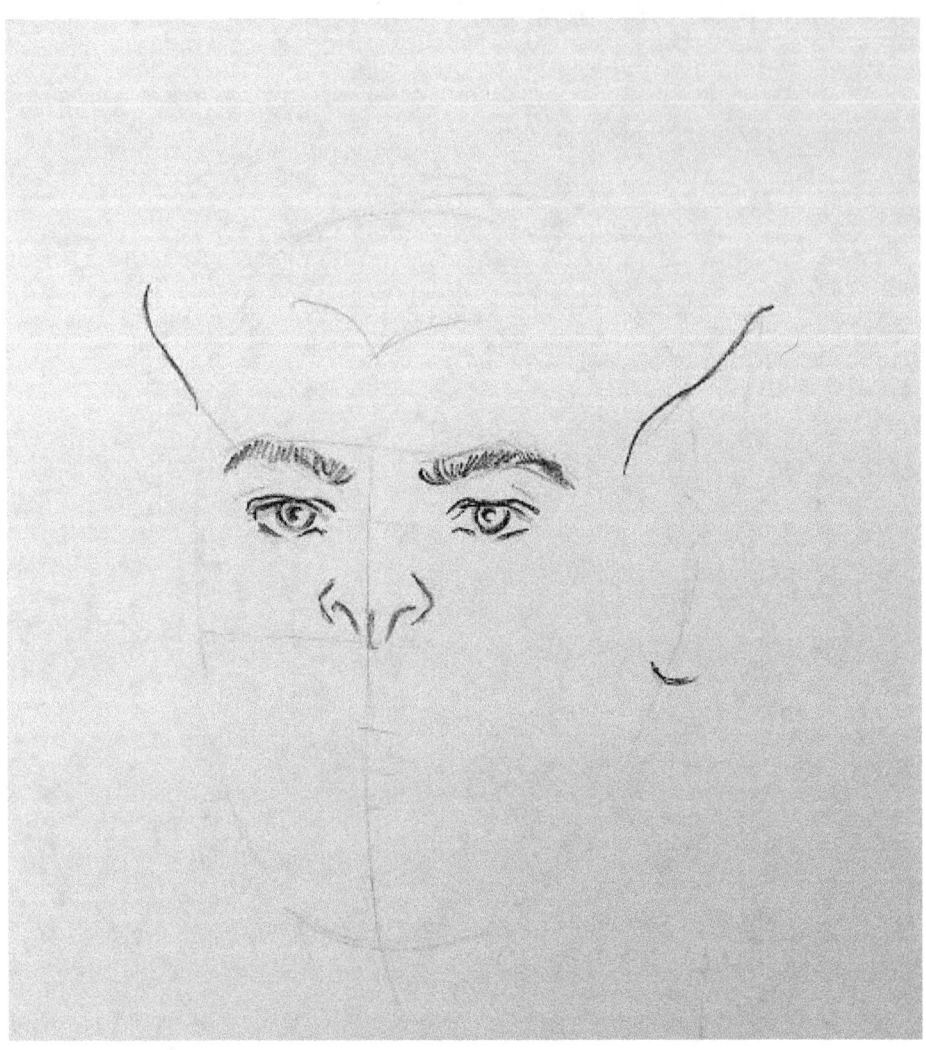

Now a little more detail. Darken the lines and add the individual hairs to the eyebrow. Figure out where the bottom of the ear will be, and darken that line as well. Finally, add the pupil and the iris to the eyes – remember that eyes shine, so there will be a little of the pupil that will seem to have a white circle over it.

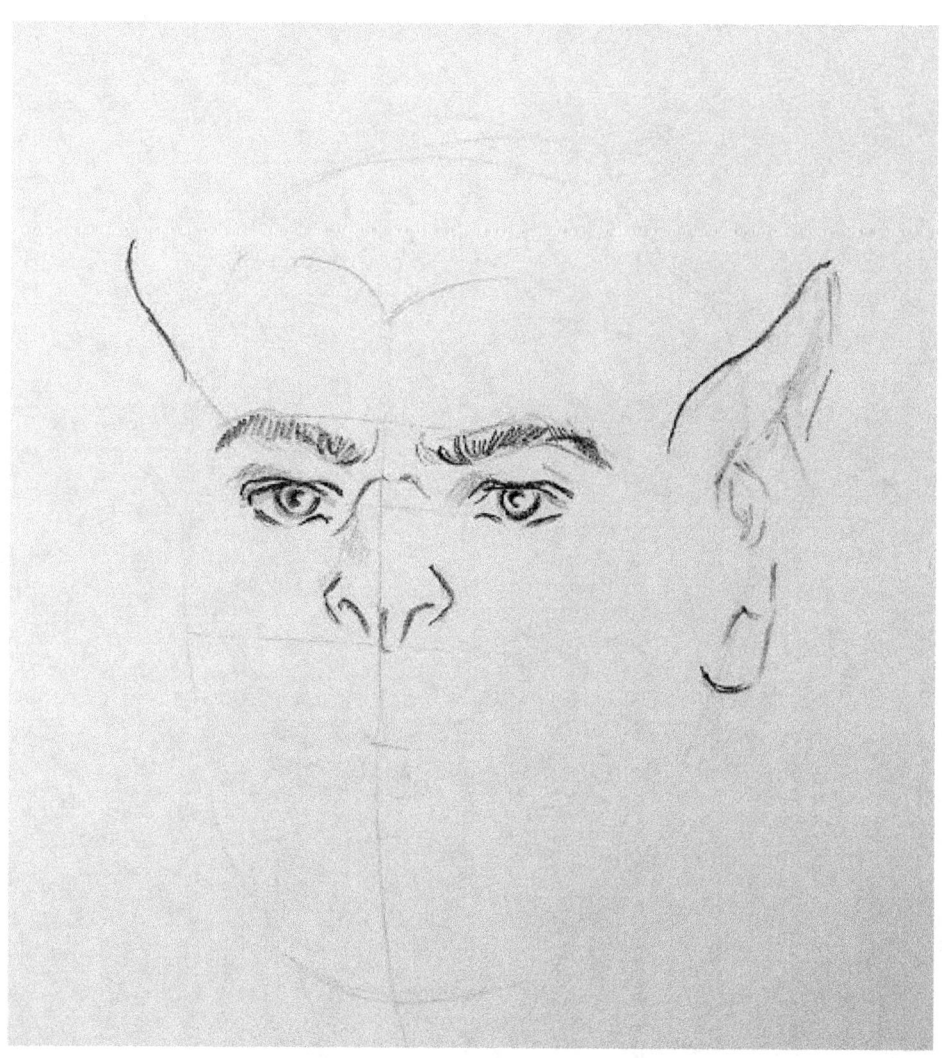

Now we're going to add a little bit of light shading to the eyes. The top of the nose will be between them, so lightly draw that in as well. When you're satisfied with the placement, darken the line. Add some detail to the ear, very lightly.

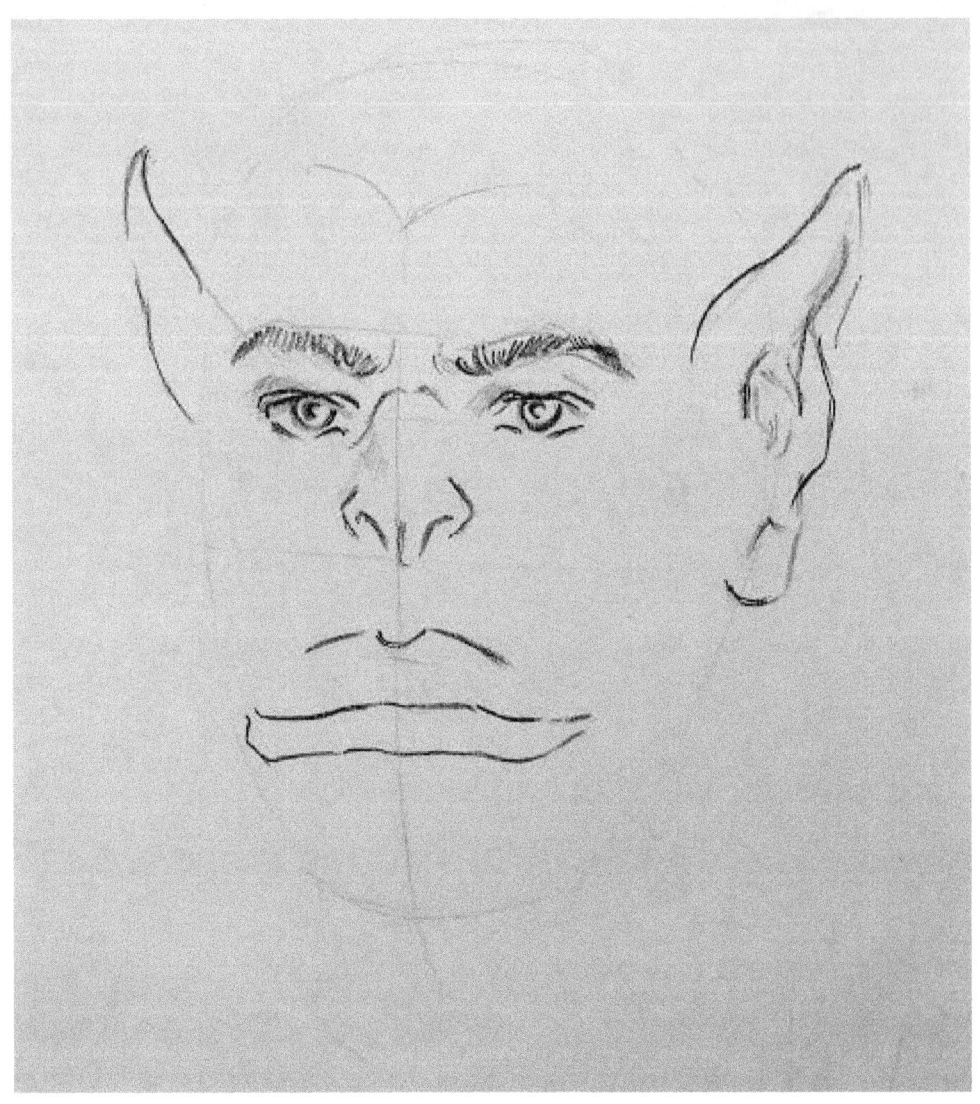

Darken the ear details and make sure you have the far ear outlined as well – the Orc can't have just one ear! Next, start outlining and darkening where the mouth will be.

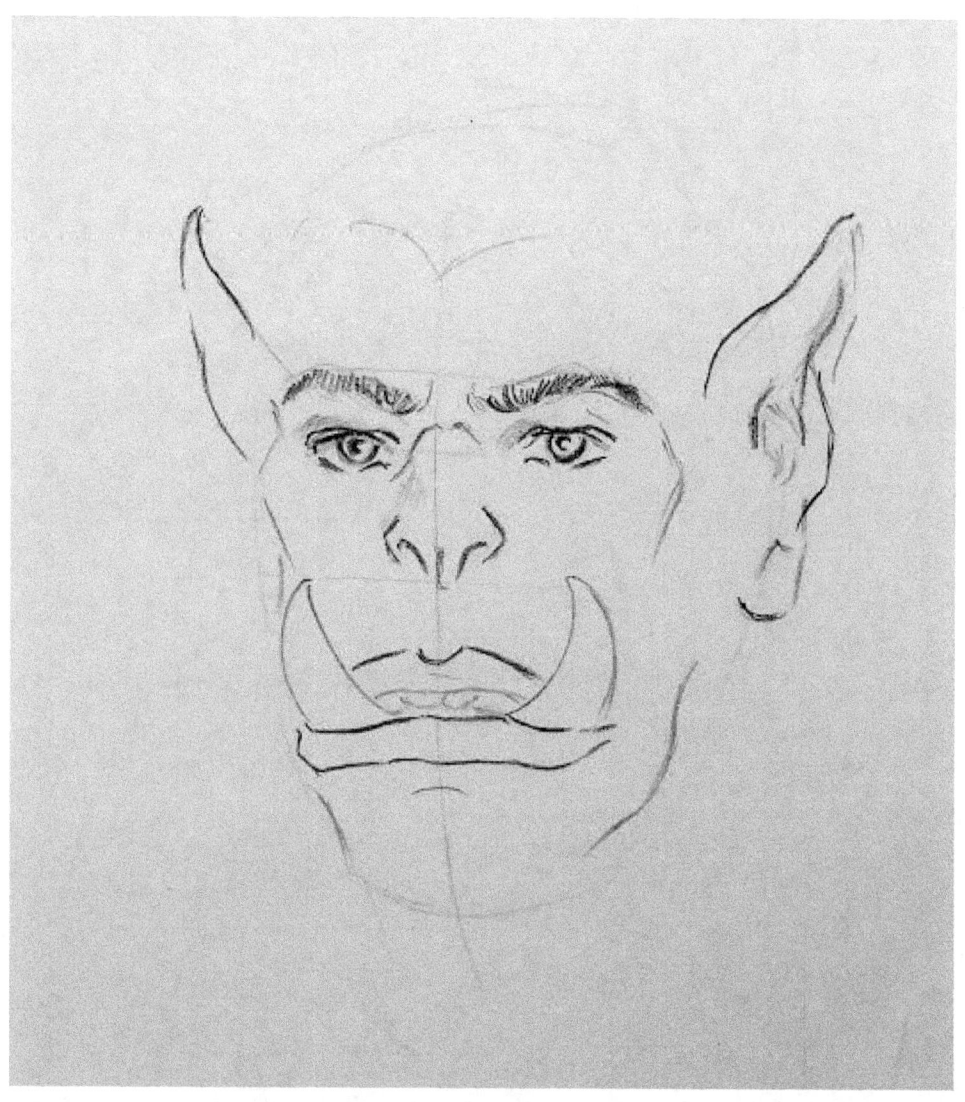

Start outlining the tusks and teeth of the Orc. The tusks are what makes an Orc look like an Orc, so be sure that you like their placement and their shape. Darken the lines of the mouth a little more.

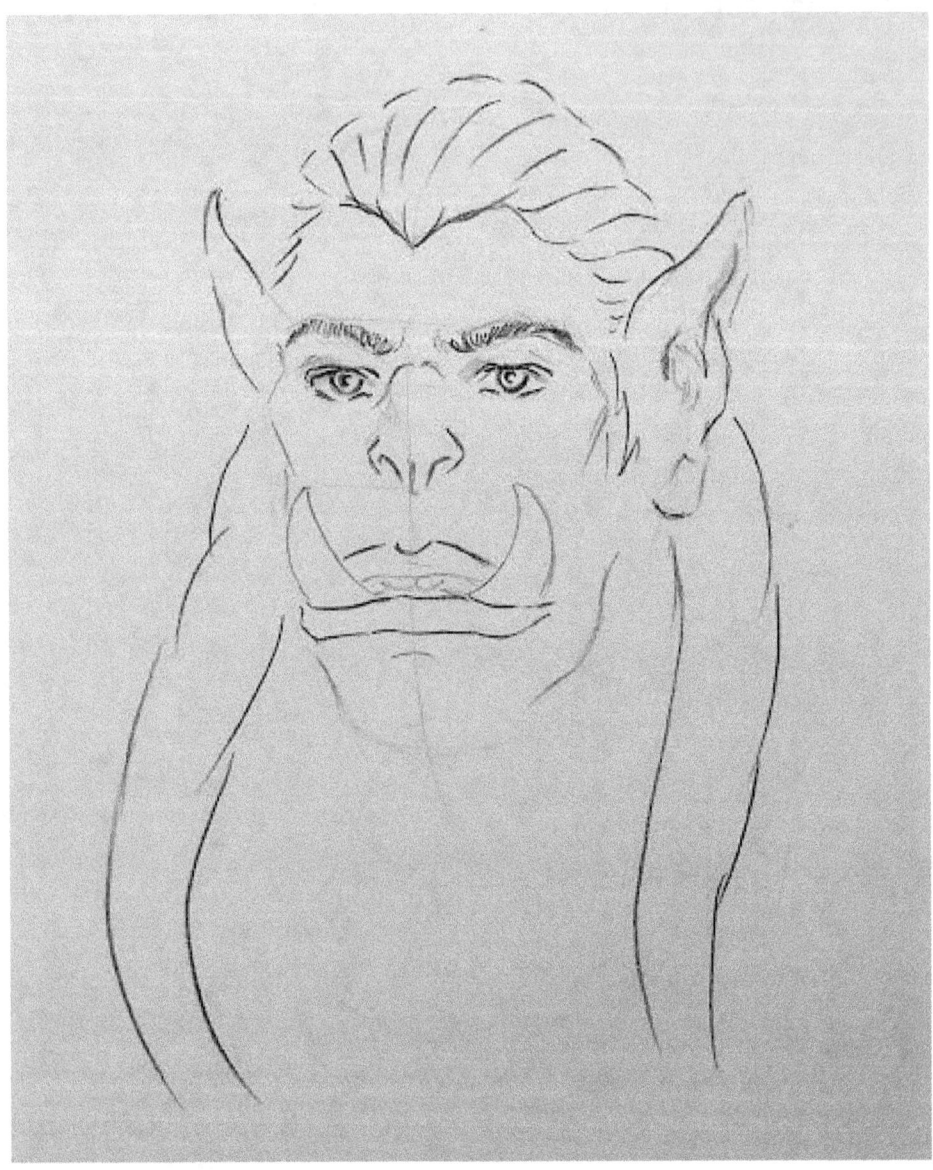

Now we're going to work on the Orc's hair. The Orc's hair is pulled into two long locks that fall over his shoulders, so we need to draw the hair sweeping back into those locks. Just do the shape of the hair for right now, we'll worry about the details later.

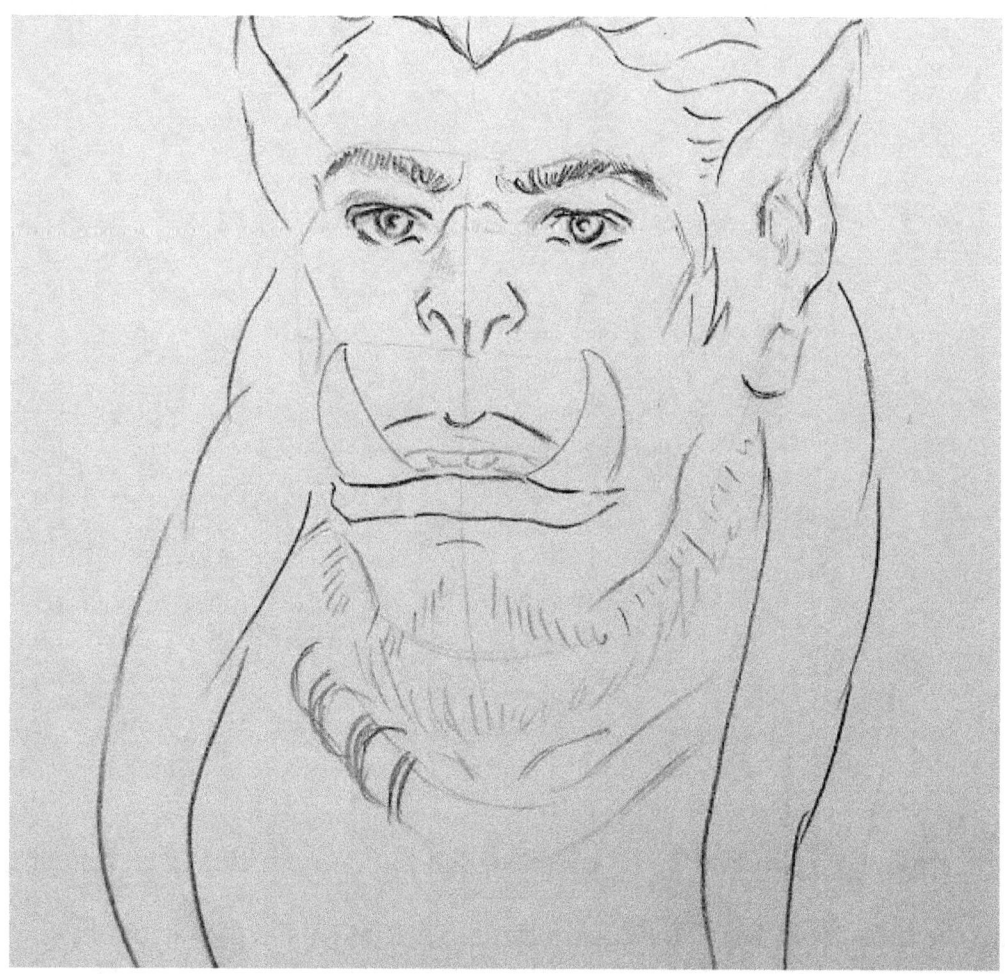

Finish off the Orc's basic face with a jaw line and a beard, as well as the beginning of the Orc's beaded necklace. Use light strokes here to give the beard a feathery appearance.

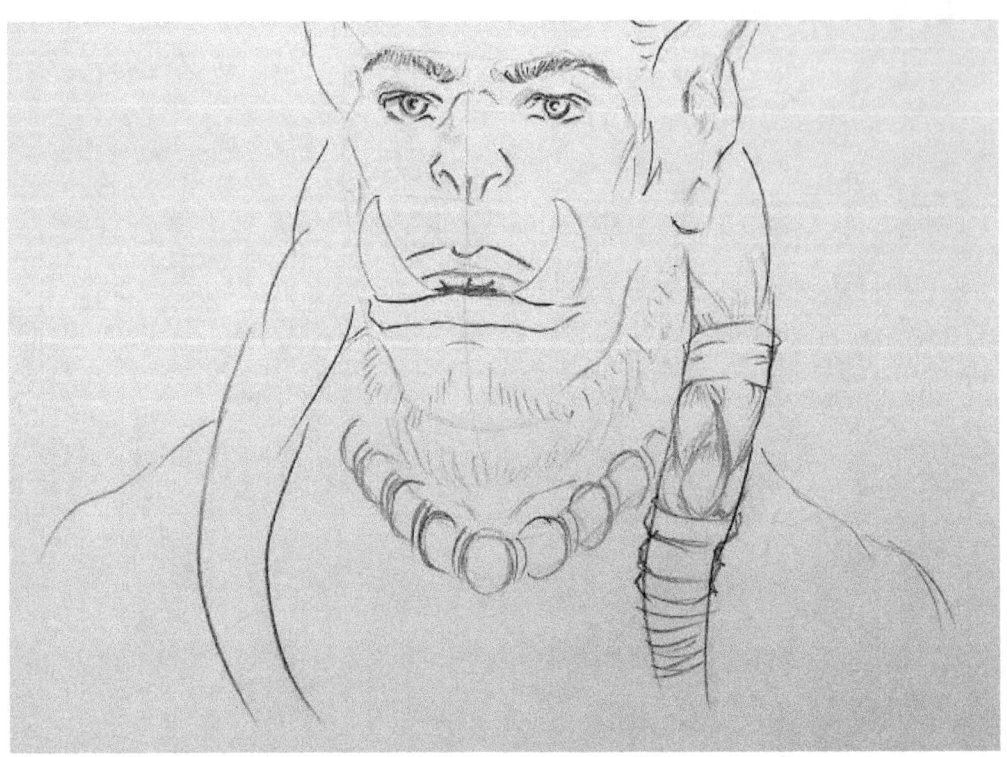

Next we're going to add some detail to the hair – specifically to the wraps and the hair itself. For the wraps, remember that this is coarse cloth, so the lines are going to be steady and kind of sharp instead of smooth and wavy like the hair. For the hair, use light strokes bunched together to give the appearance of individual strands.

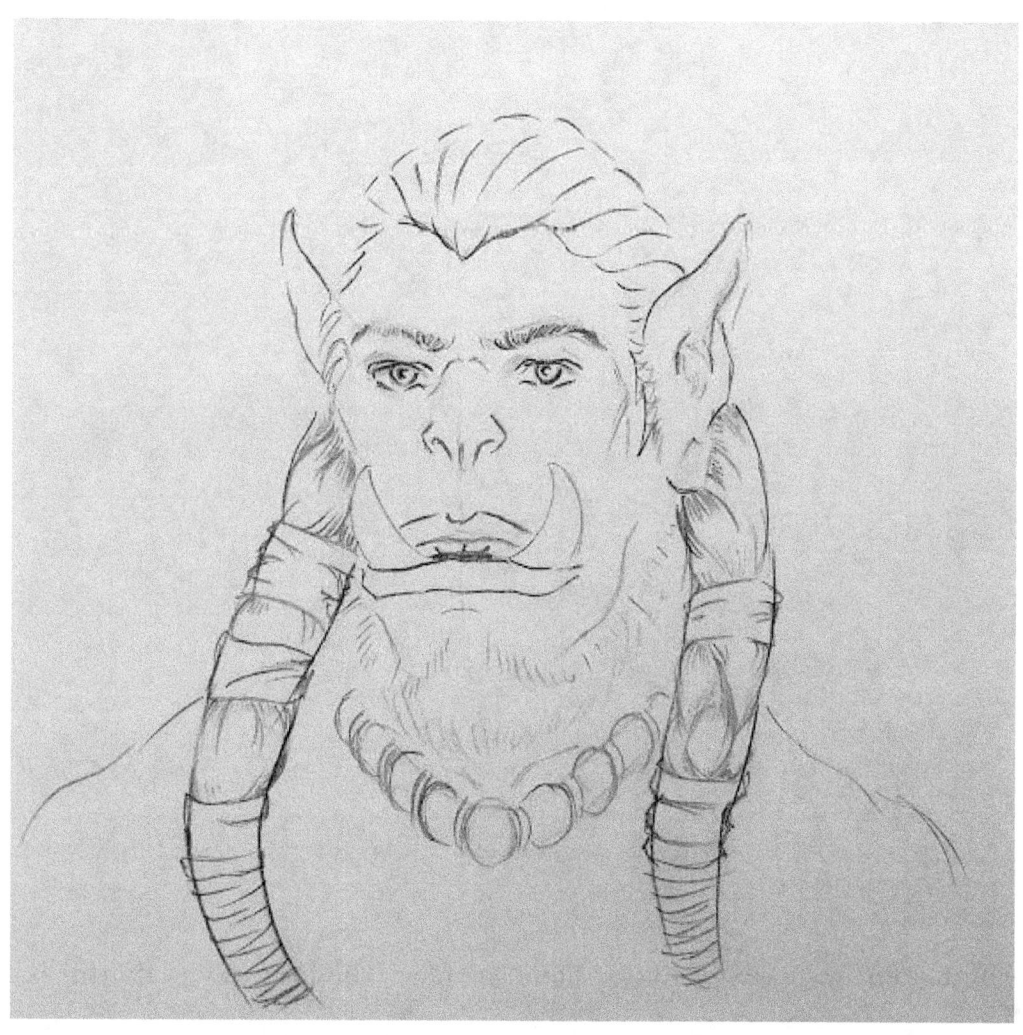

Finish off the detail of the hair and the wraps, using the same method of sharp lines for the wraps and soft, bunched lines for the hair.

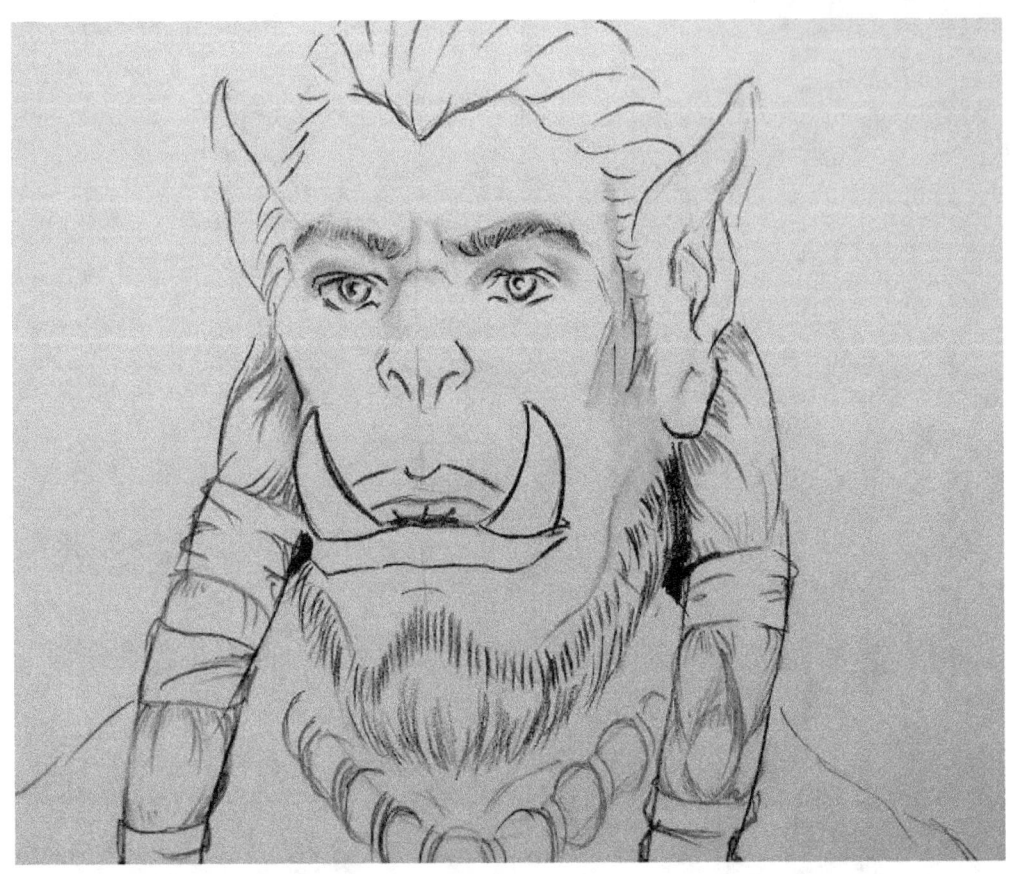

Darken your lines and begin to shade the face. The best way to do this is to lightly draw lines and then smudge them, either with a smudging tool or with your finger. Smudge them the way that you want it shaded, adding lines and erasing them as you go.

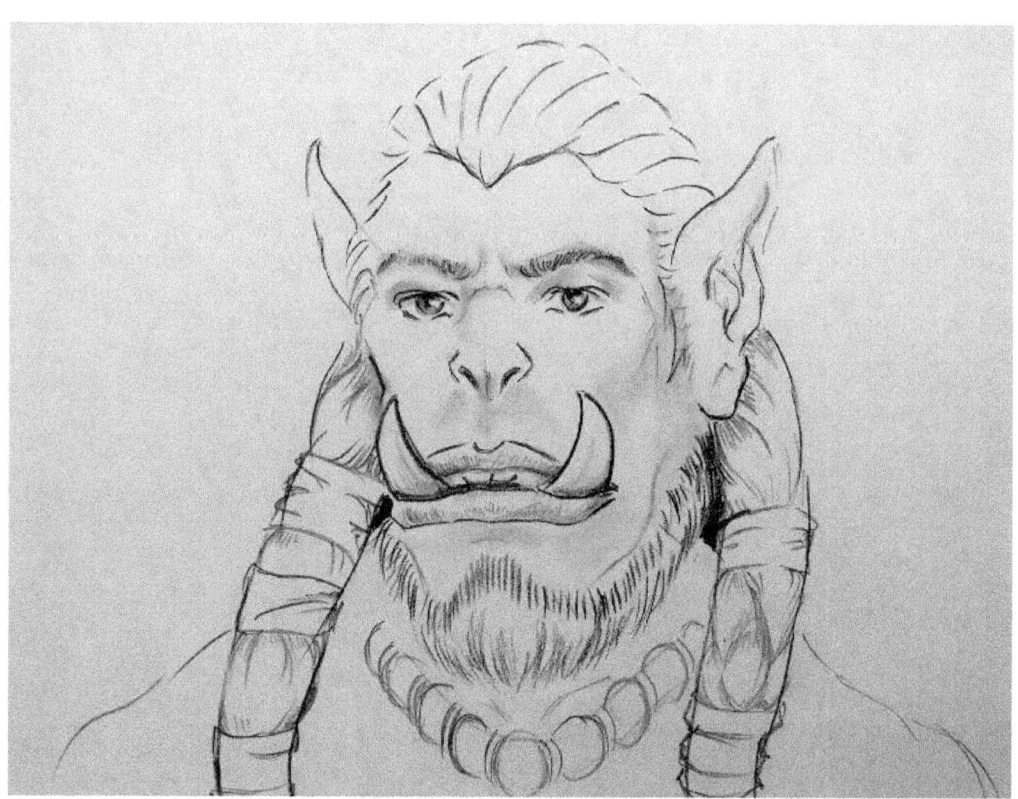

Continue shading the face, and then add some detail to the lips and the beaded necklace. Shade the tusks a little, as well as the teeth. The inside of the Orc's mouth is going to be dark, so don't be afraid of pressure here.

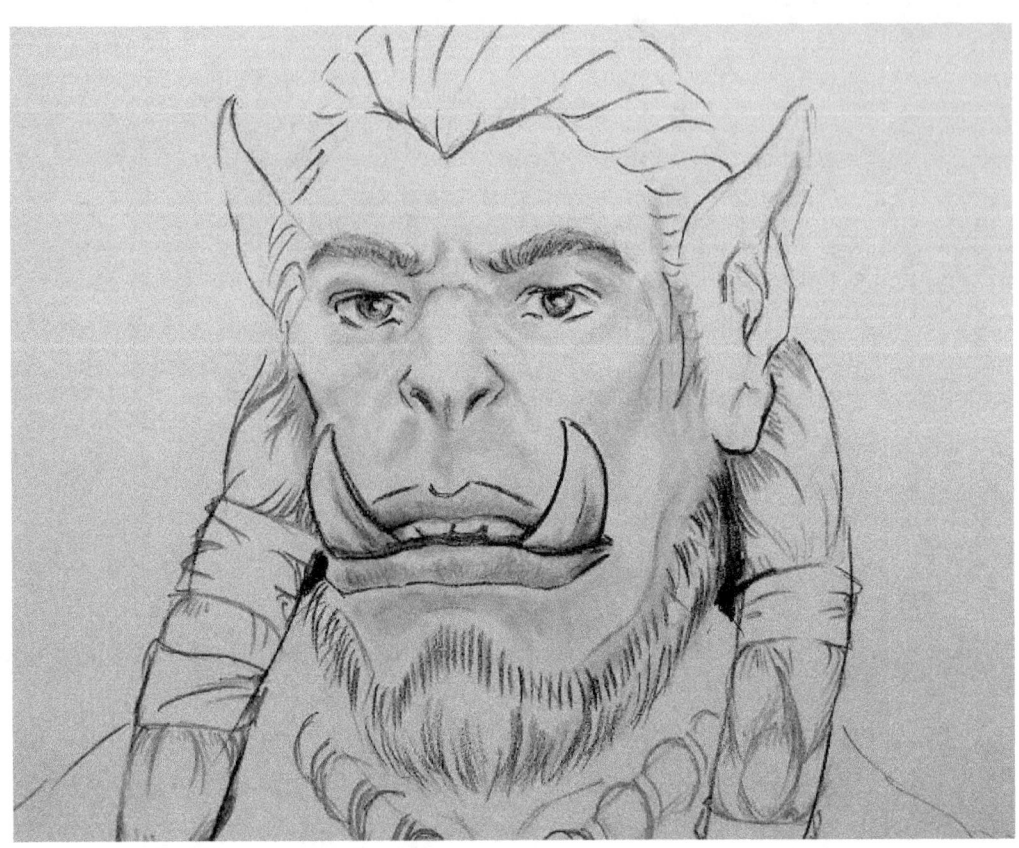

Smudge the lines you just did on the lips very carefully. This gives the Orc a smoother, more polished look.

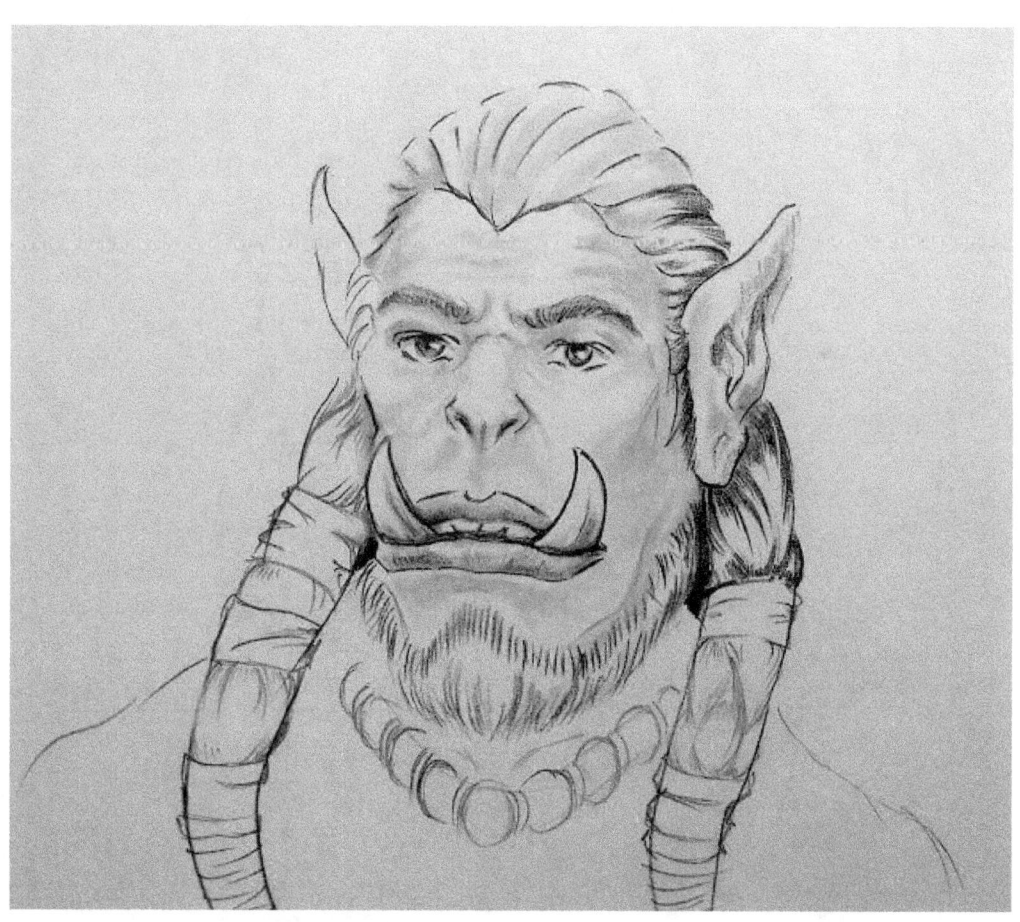

Now start shading the hair and the forehead, using the same smudging method for the top of the hair. For the bottom, we want the individual strands to stand out, so don't be afraid of pressure or strong lines as you work on the shading.

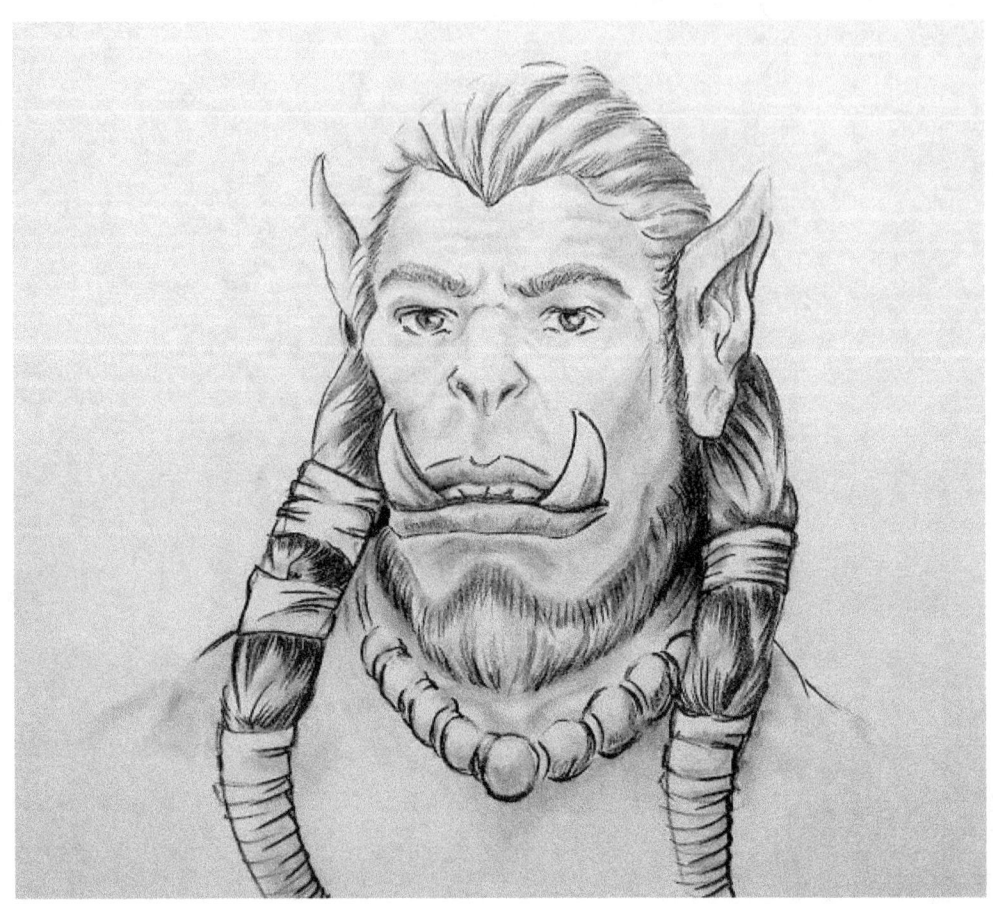

Continue shading the hair and the wraps, as well as the beaded necklace.
Smudge a little bit, but not as much as you did with the face – we want the
dark strands of hair to stand out.

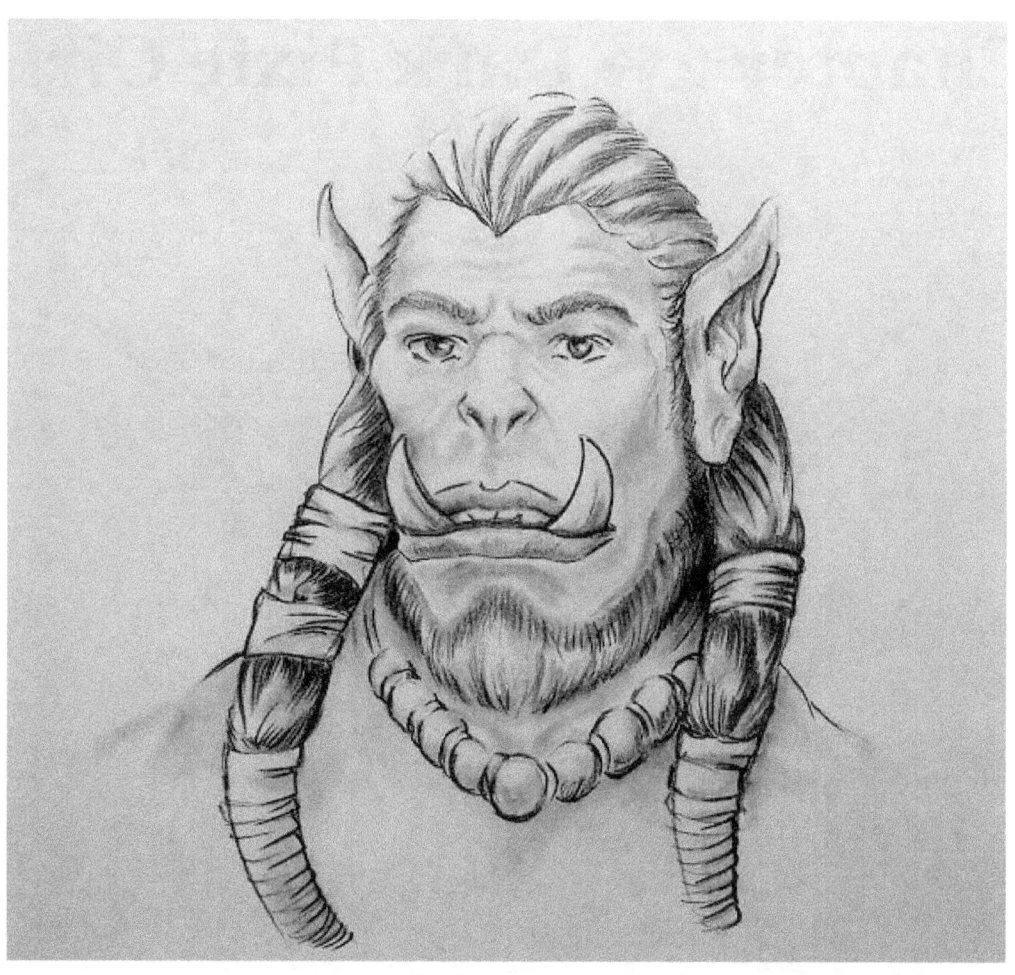

And you're done! Your Orc is ready to offer advice to your hero or plunder and pillage a village – your choice.

Chapter 2 – Dark Pixie Girl

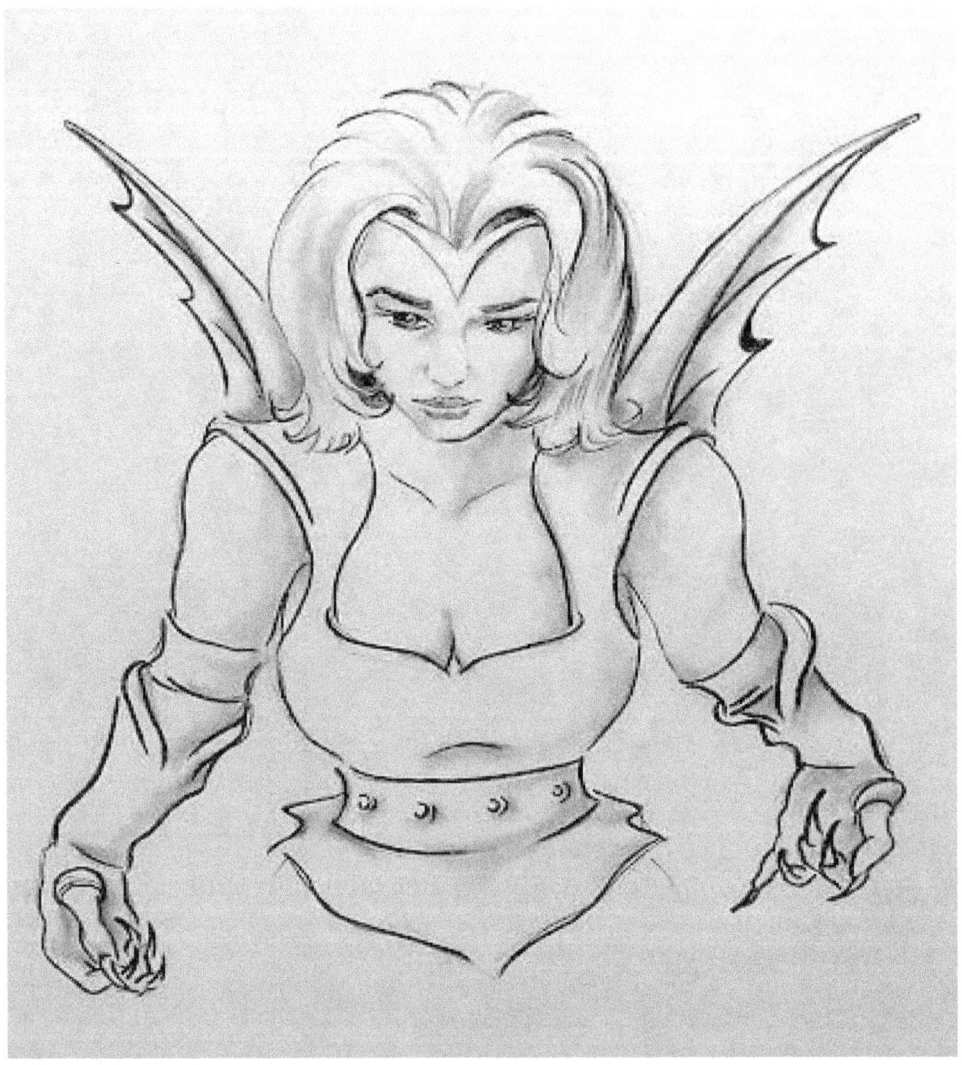

The dark pixie girl is an interesting character when it comes to fantasy. She can either be a villain or a misunderstood ally, and she is a ton of fun to draw. With claws that curve and wings that are beautifully dark, the dark pixie girl is ready to either help or hurt you – your choice.

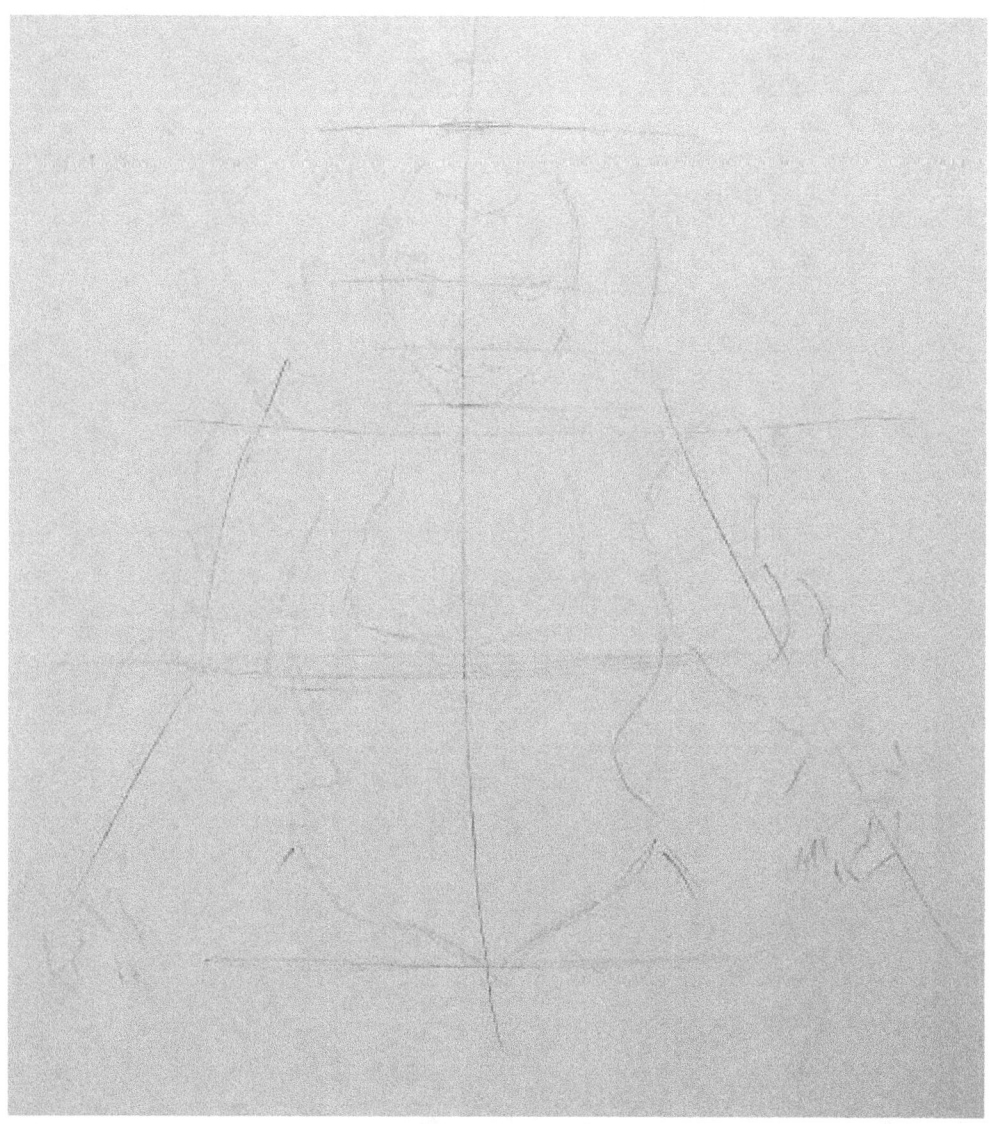

Start by laying out the very basics of the dark pixie girl. Draw lines to indicate the movement of the body and the arms, as well as where her chest, waist, shoulders, eyes, and nose is. This outline will serve to guide us through the rest of the drawing.

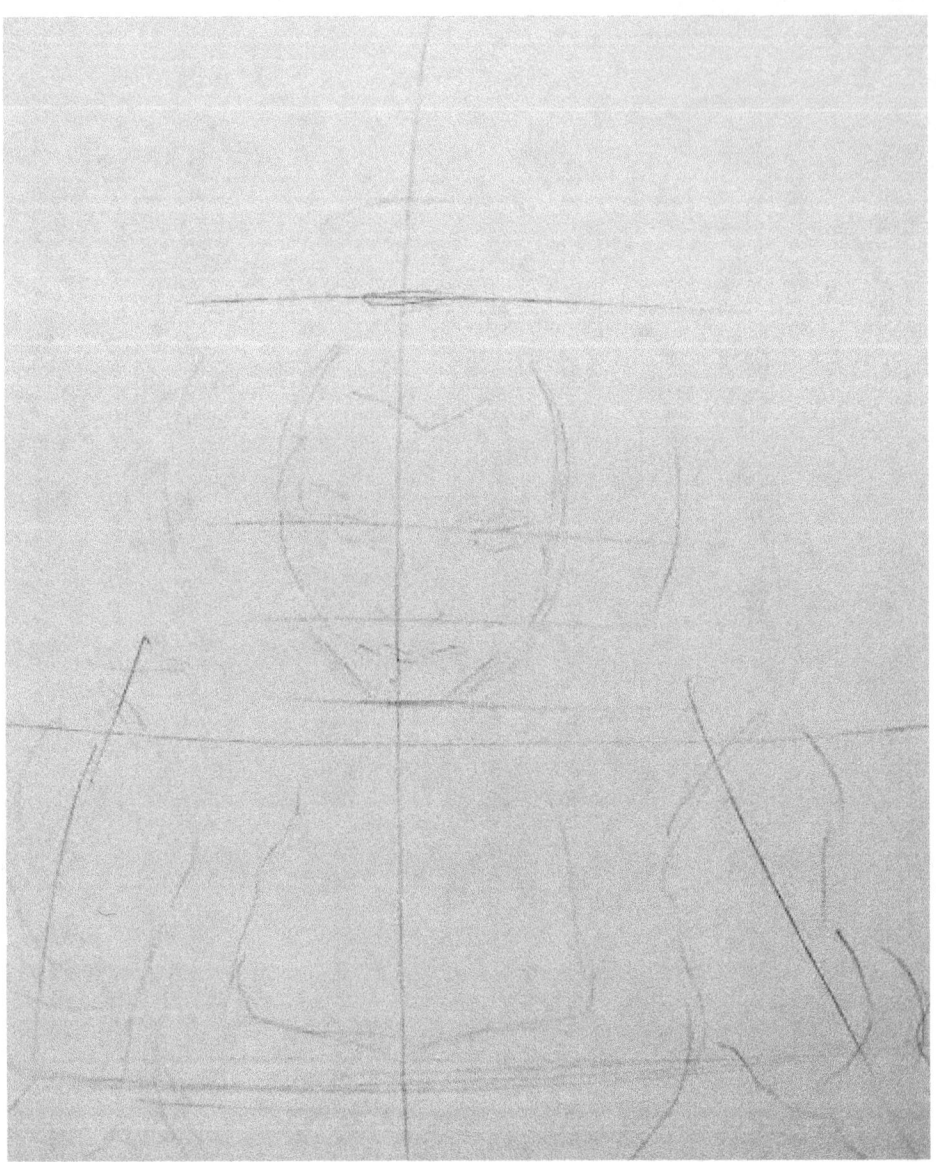

Add a little bit of detail into the face, where the eyes will go, the hairline, and the nose and mouth. Also, add an outline as to where you would like the hair to go out to.

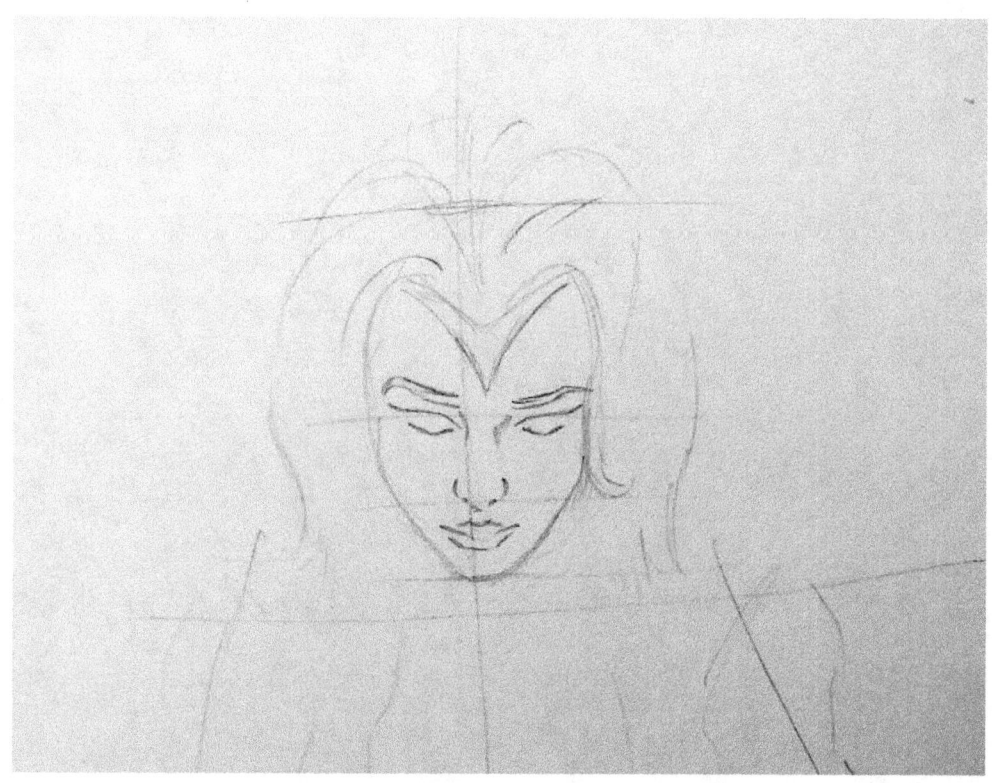

Now we're going to add even more detail to the face. Use a harder pressure or a darker pencil, and add the outline details of the face – the lines of the eyes, nose and lips, as well as of the circlet and the hair. Don't go too dark here – just dark enough.

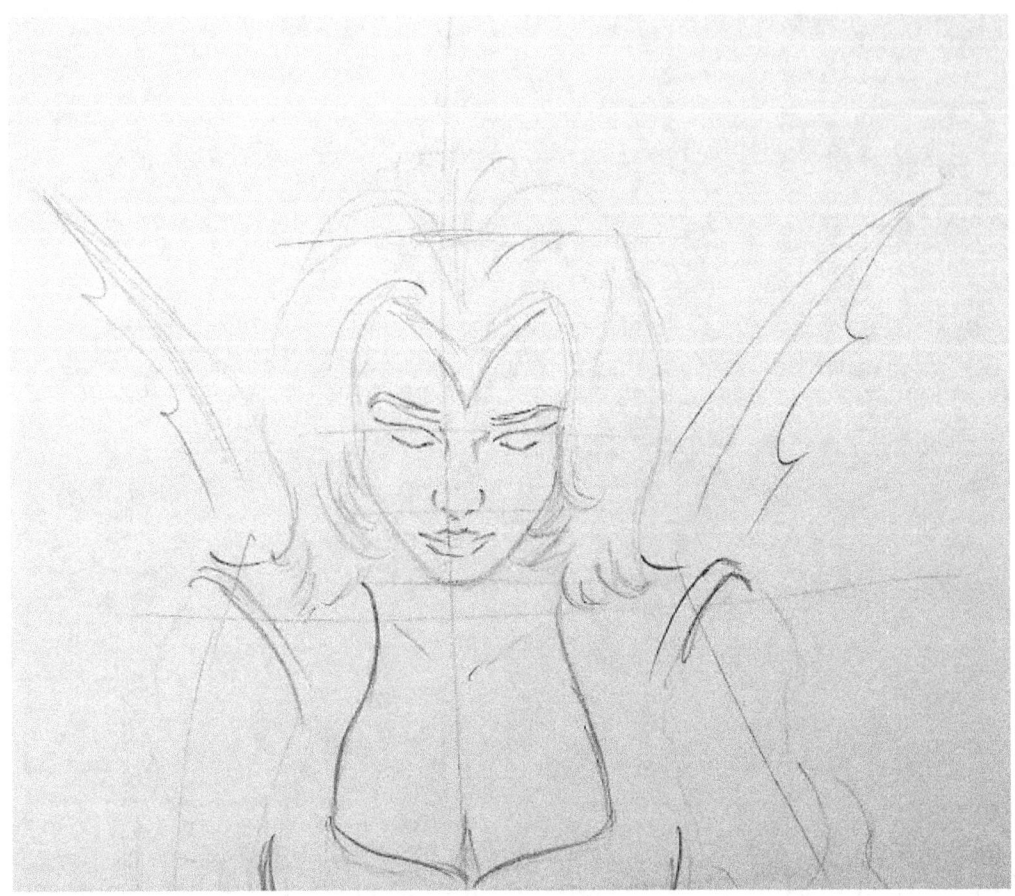

Now we're going to start darkening the lines of the wings, the shoulders, and the cleavage, as well as finishing up the outline of the hair. Notice the difference in pressure between the hair and the dark outlines – we want the hair to flow, whereas the outlines are lines that don't move the way that hair does.

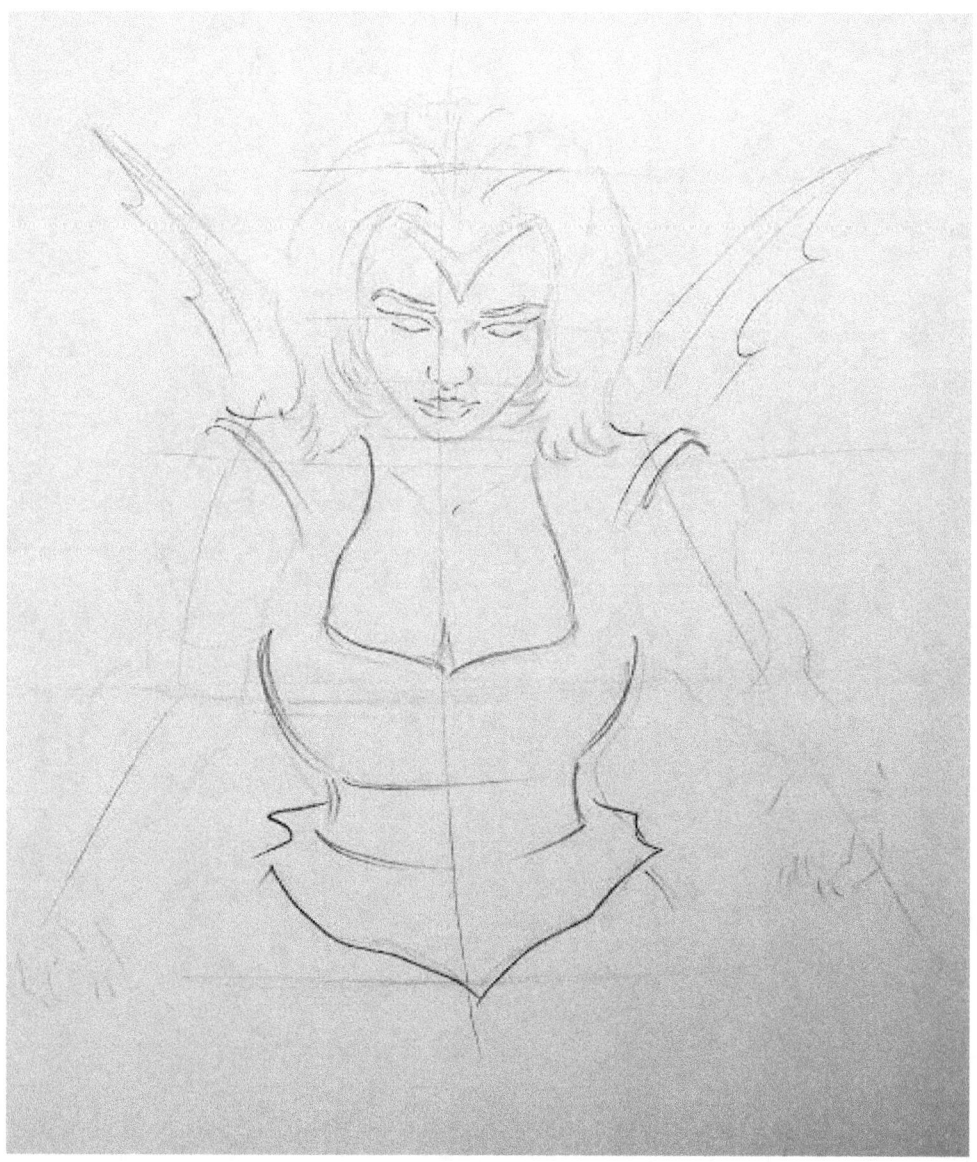

Finish up outlining the outfit; add some light details to the arms – the curve of the fingers, for example, or how you want the wrists to twist.

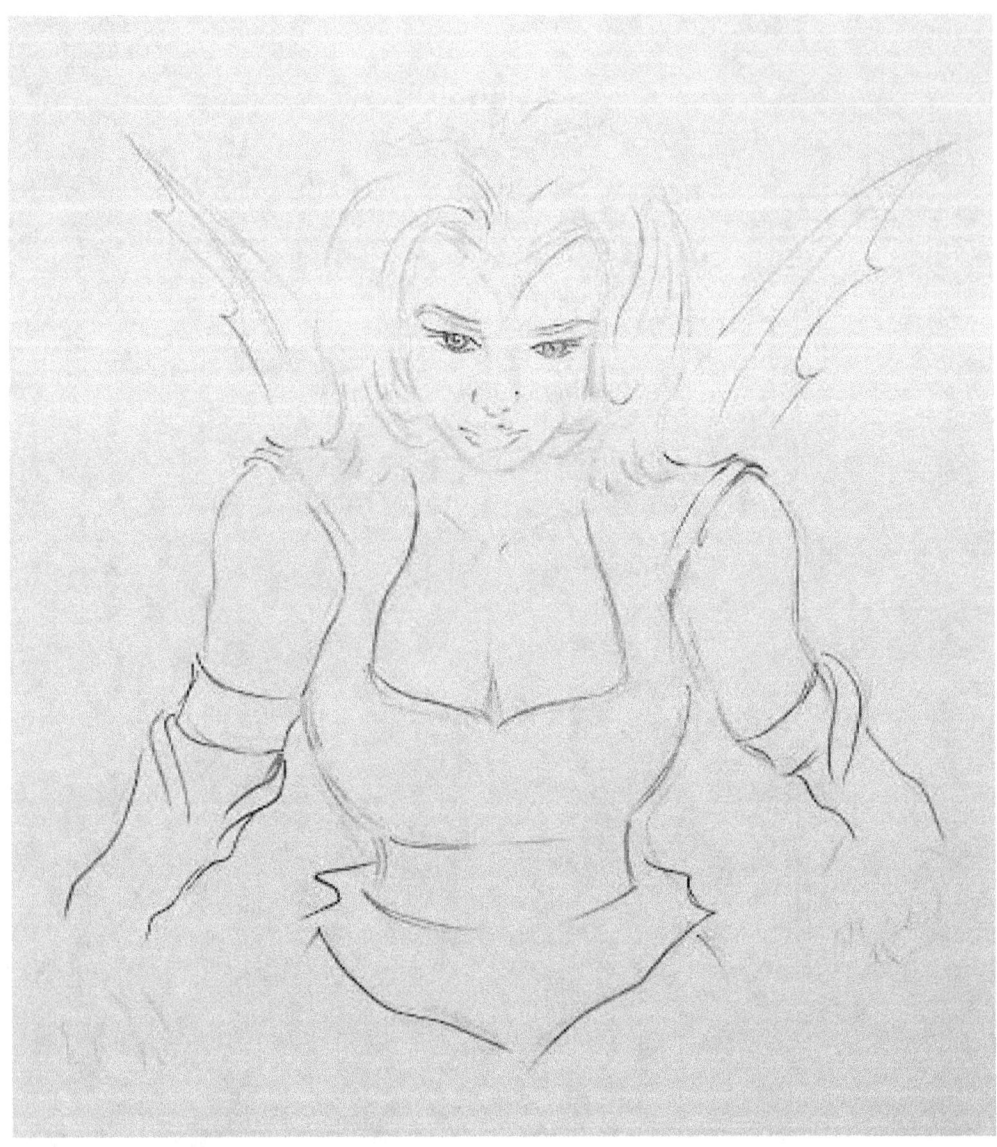

Now we're going to add the pupil and iris to the eye. Remember that the

pupil will have a little white circle in it to represent how shiny the eye is.

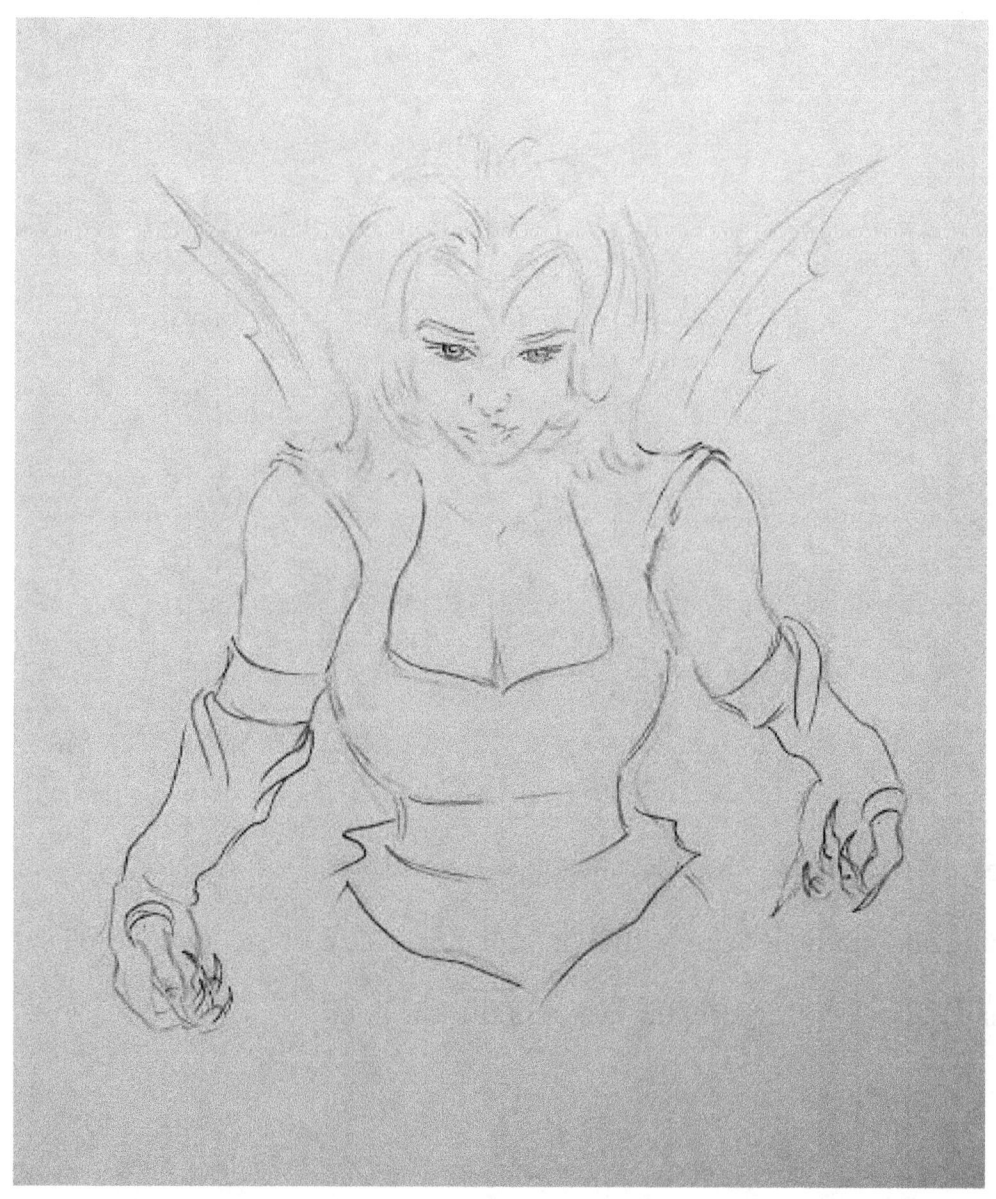

Now we're going to finalize the arm and hand lines. We want the claws to curve, but we want it to be a natural curve. Don't be afraid of pressure for these lines.

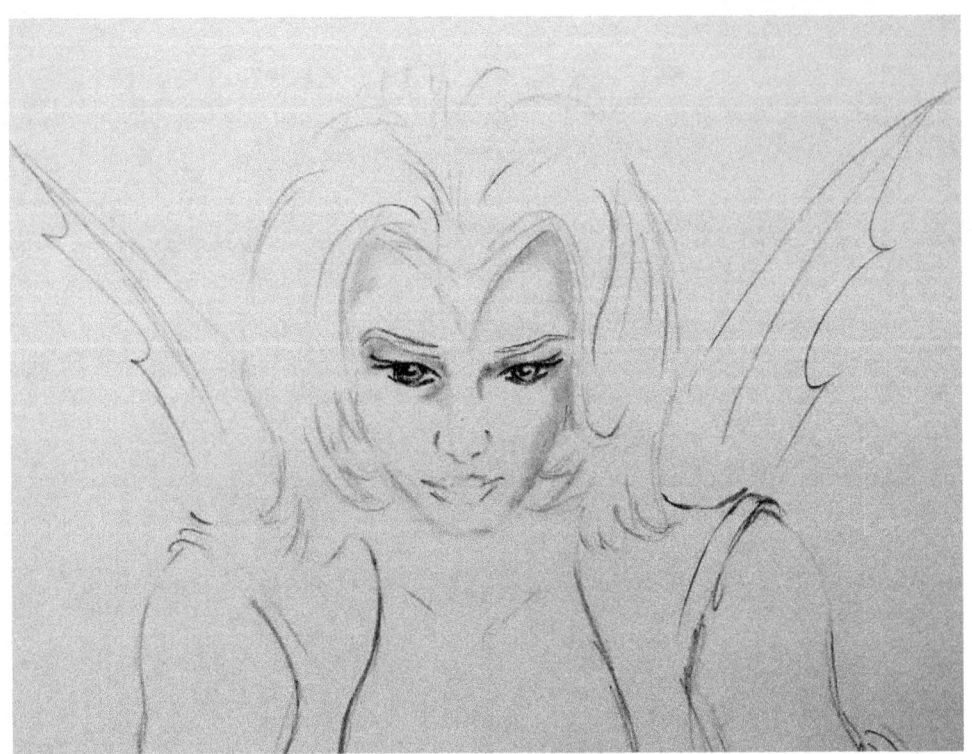

Then we can start shading! Just like we did with the Orc, use the same smudging method, using a tool or your finger. These are going to be softer shades, however, around the eyes and the hairline.

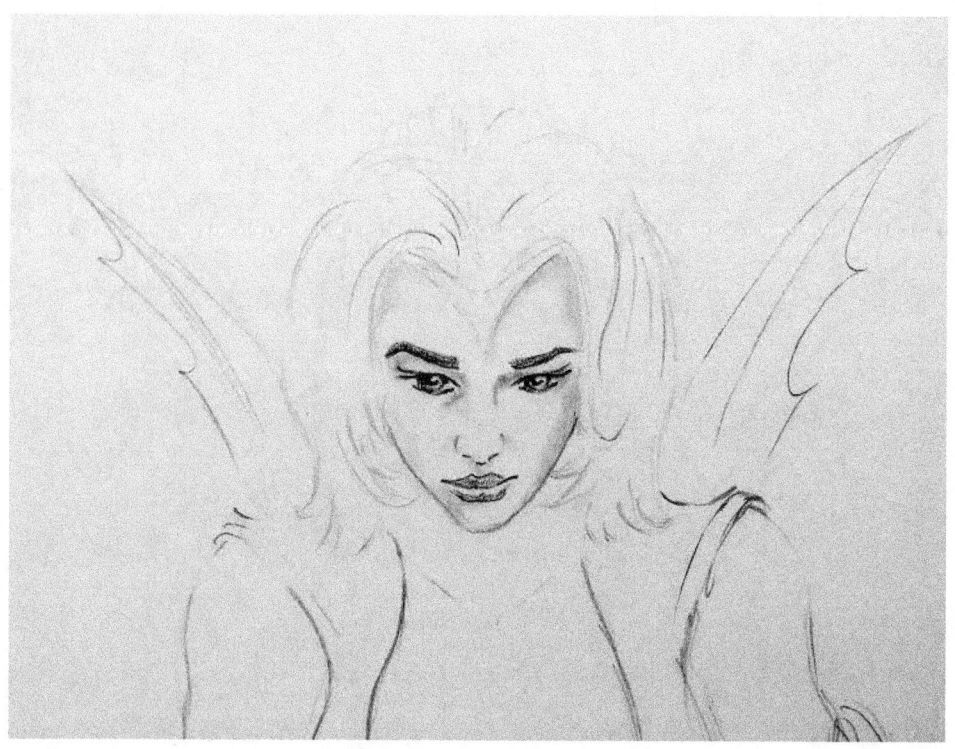

Add detail to the lip – lots of little lines bunched together. The gap between the lips represents the shine of her lips, like she's wearing gloss or lipstick.

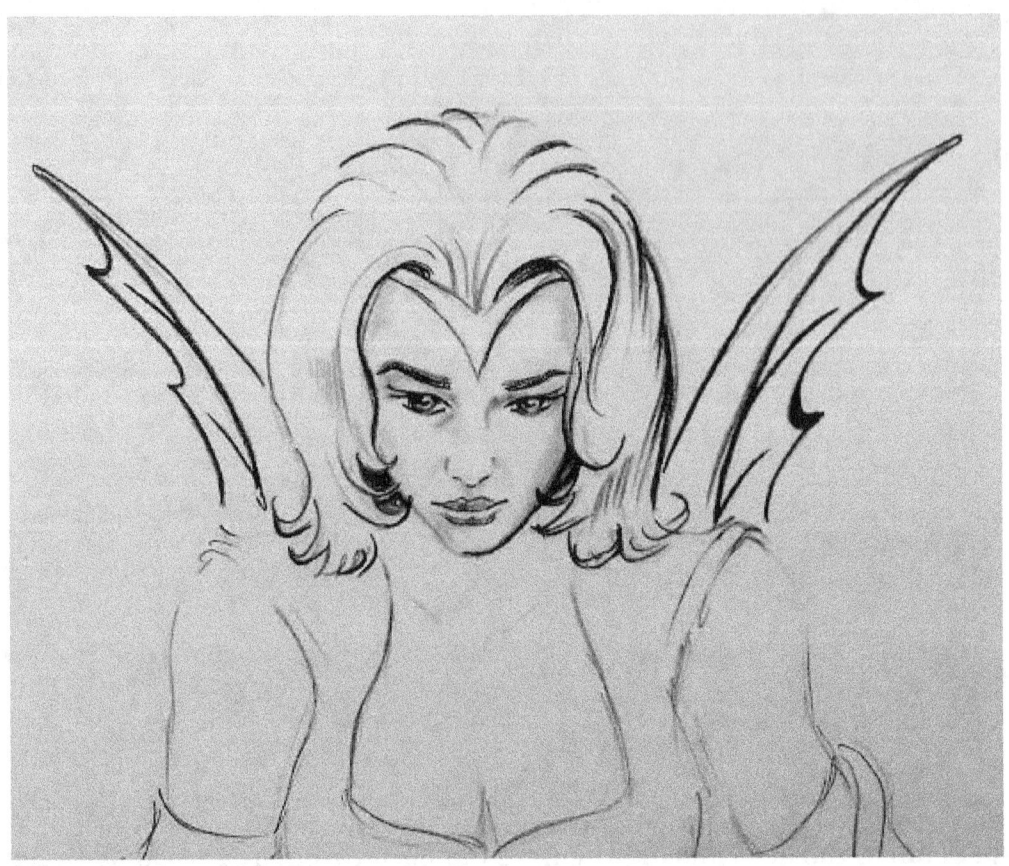

Now we're going to start darkening lines and shading the hair. Remember for the hair we want to use lighter lines than everything else, as we want to give it a soft appearance.

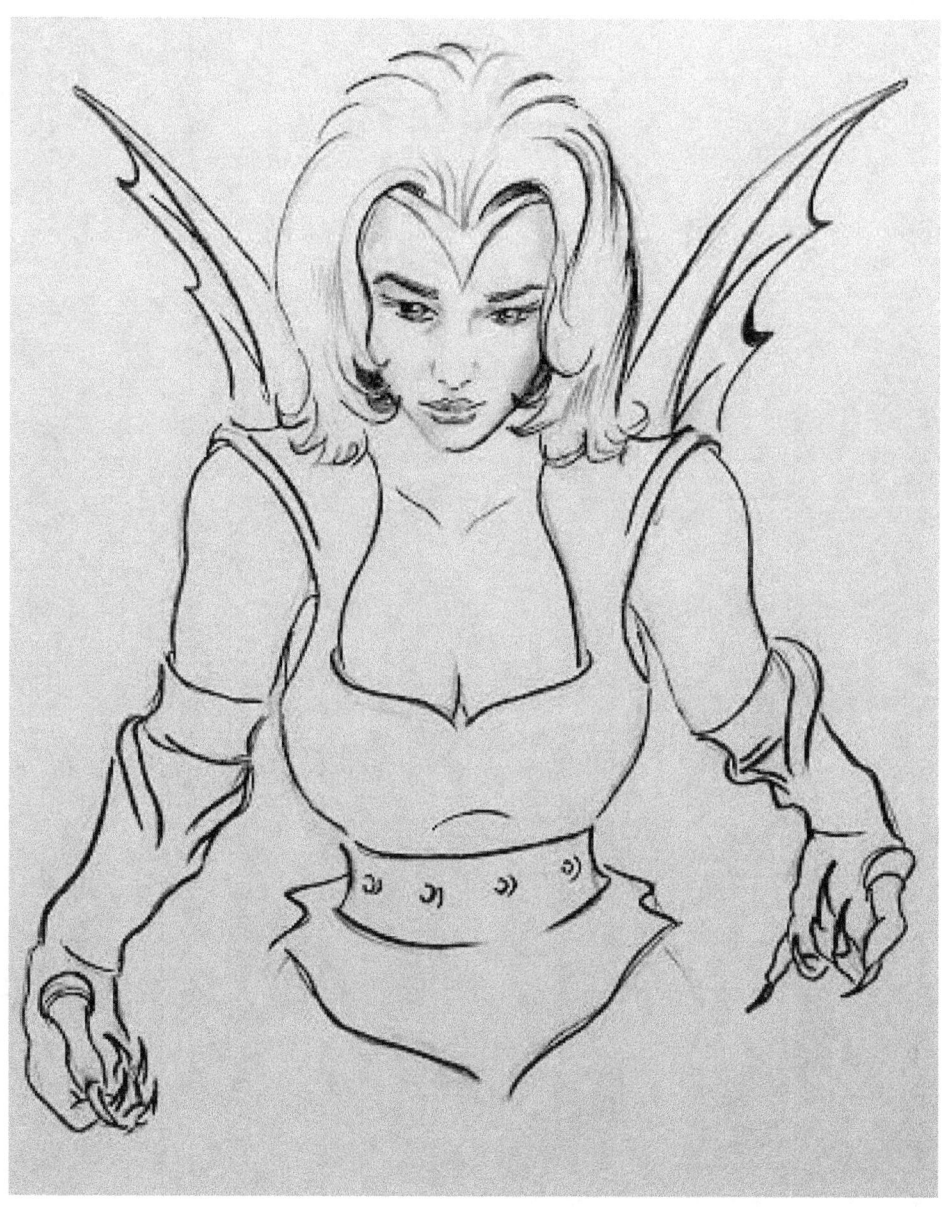

Darken the lines across the image.

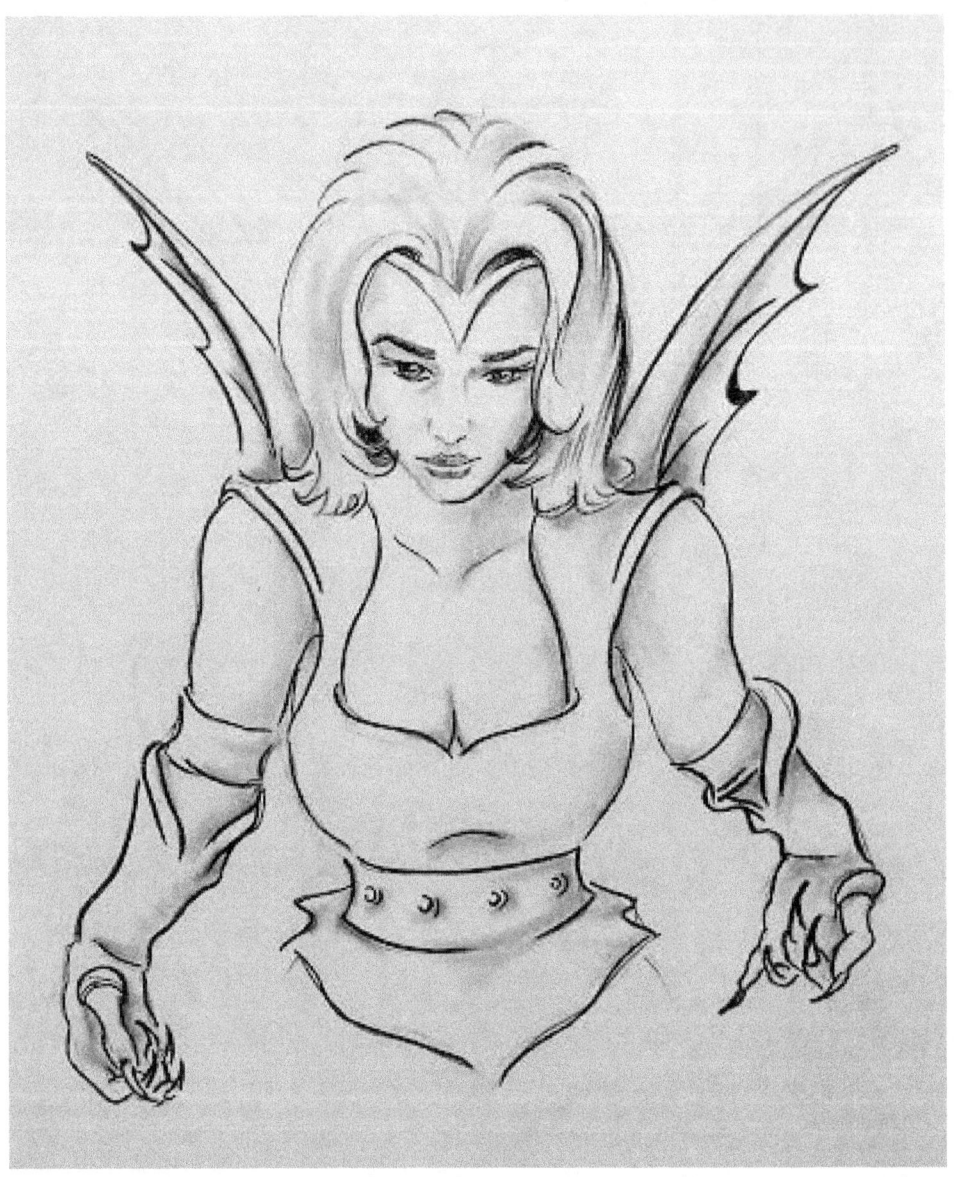

Start doing some shading, using the same smudging method that we have

been using. Remember where your light source is and shade accordingly.

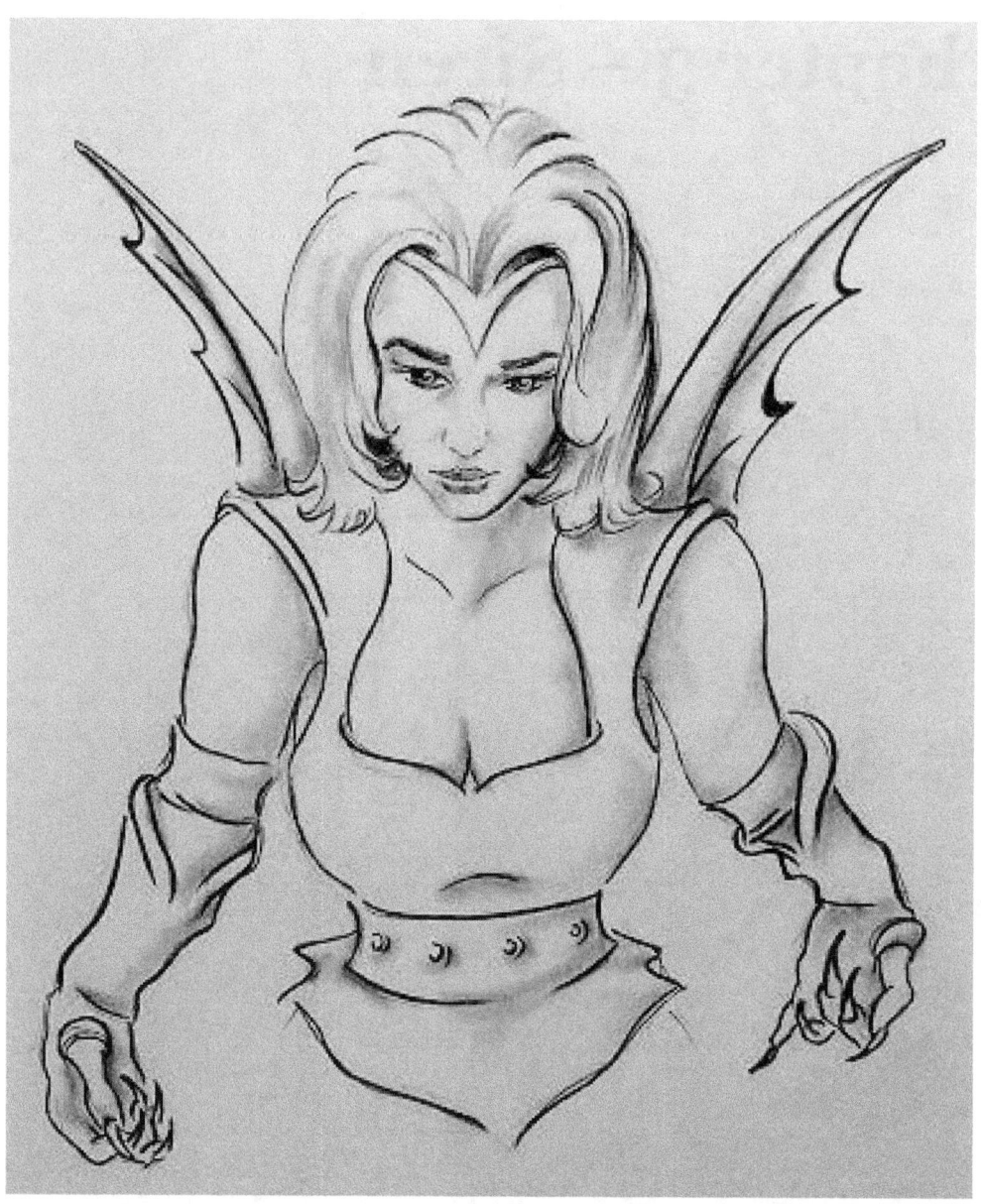

Then you should have a final Dark Pixie Girl, ready to wreak havoc or help

out your hero in a roundabout, confusing way.

Chapter 3 – Siren

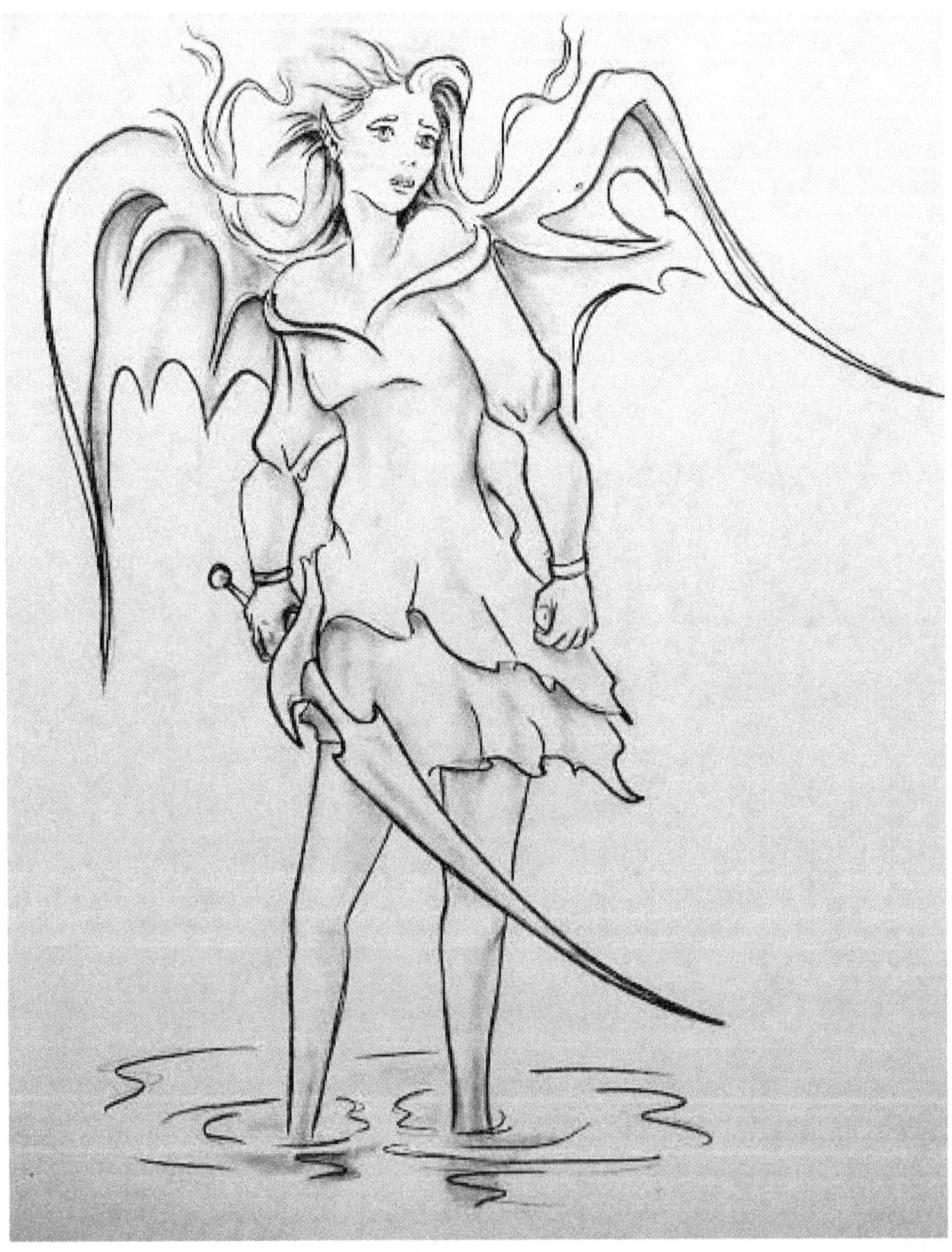

Sirens use their beauty and charm to lure their prey in, hypnotize them with their song, and then kill them. This siren is ready to find her next victim – could it be your hero?

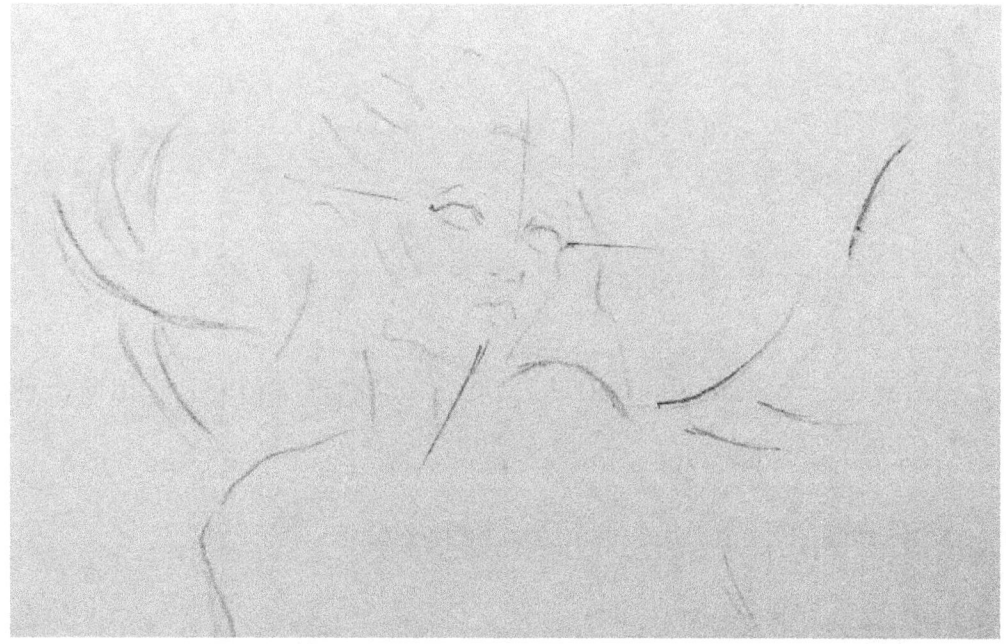

Start by placing the outlines down of the face, shoulders, and wings. Do a little bit of the detail of the face – where the eyes, nose and mouth will go – as well as for the hair.

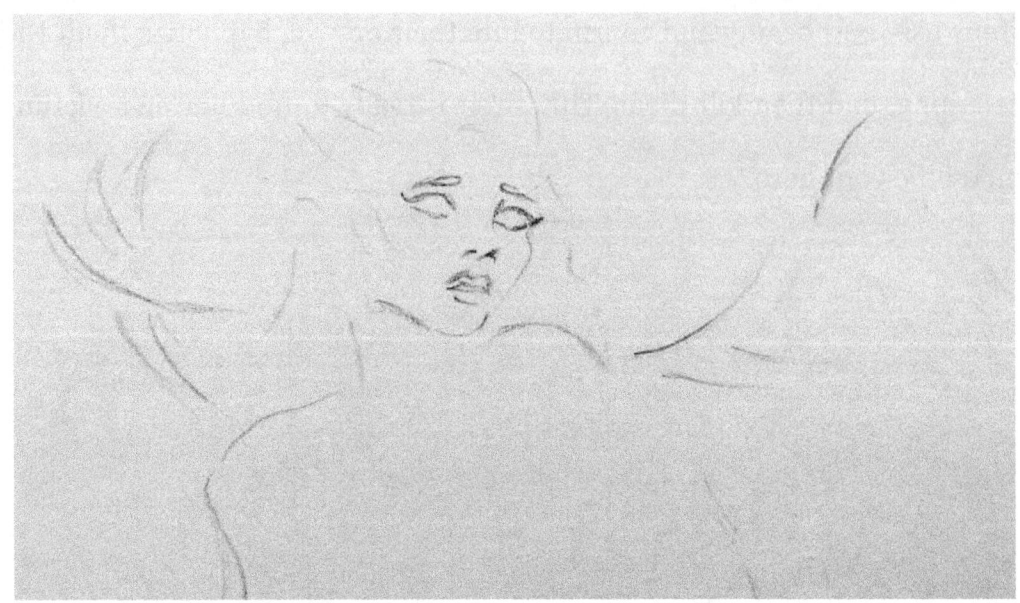

Get a little bit more detailed. Erase your guidelines and get a little darker with your pencil. She's got a forlorn expression, as though she hates what her nature makes her do and wishes to be free of it.

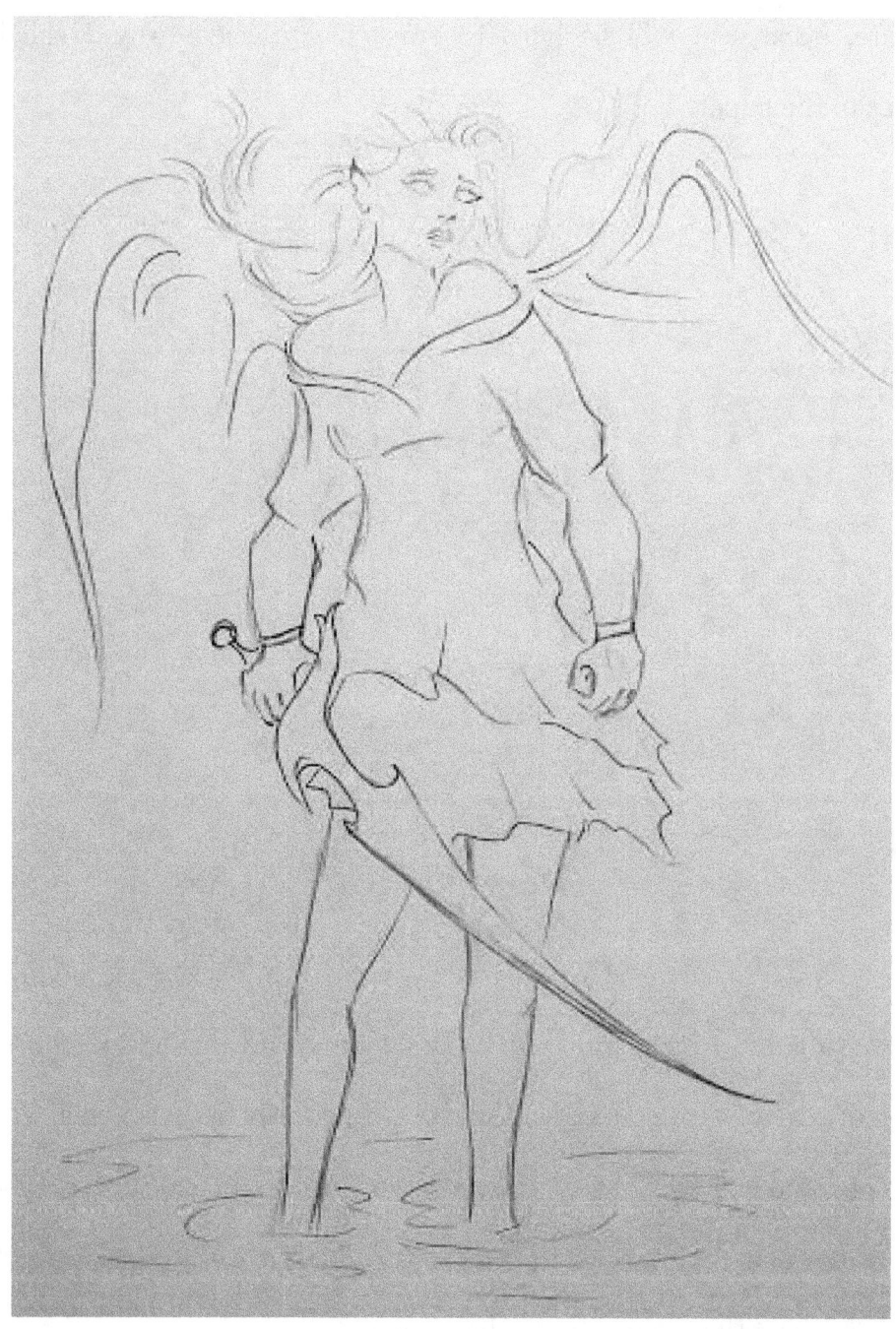

Do the outlines for the rest of the body, the sword, and the water. Do the

first lines lightly, and then use darker lines – don't start out with a lot of pressure, because it will be hard to erase if you need to and will leave grooves in the paper.

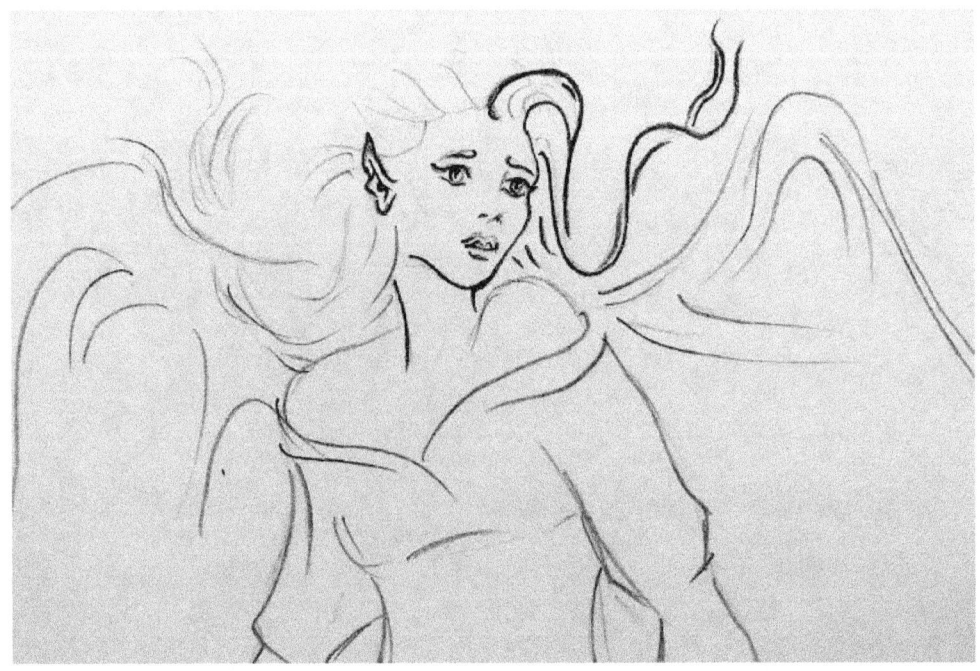

Now we're going to get really dark! Don't be afraid of pressure here, but make sure that you've already done the details in lighter pencil so that you're absolutely sure where you want your lines to go. Add the pupils and irises of the eyes, and let her hair flow as though it were underwater, even though she isn't (it's totally part of her magic).

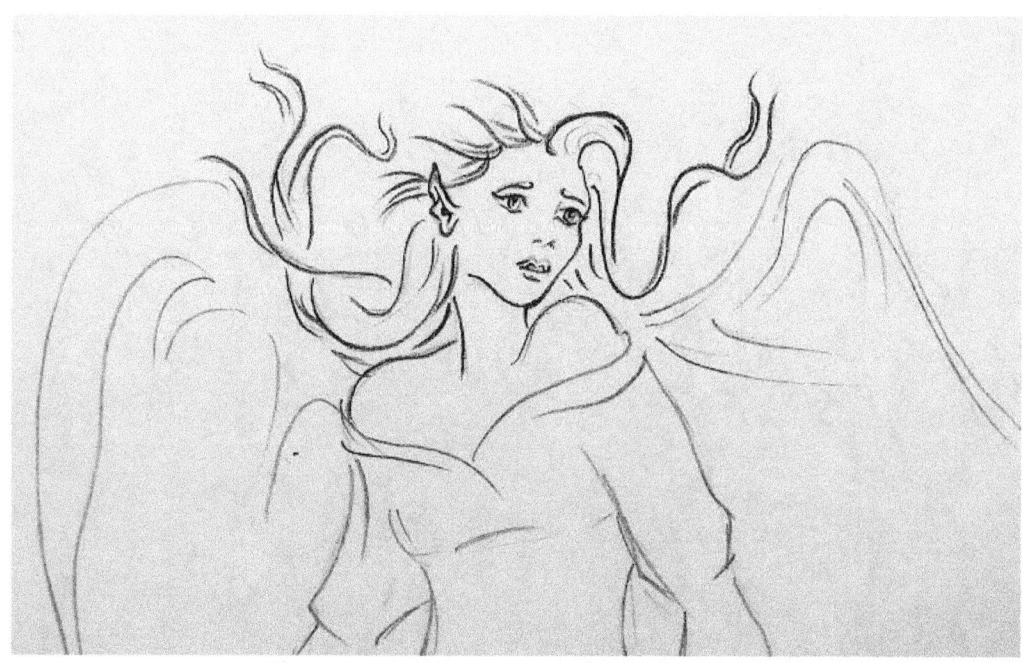

Finish outlining the hair – we want flowing, steady lines, so take your time and don't rush. Doesn't worry about letting the lines fade a little at the end, as it will look like the strand gets smaller and smaller before the hair ends.

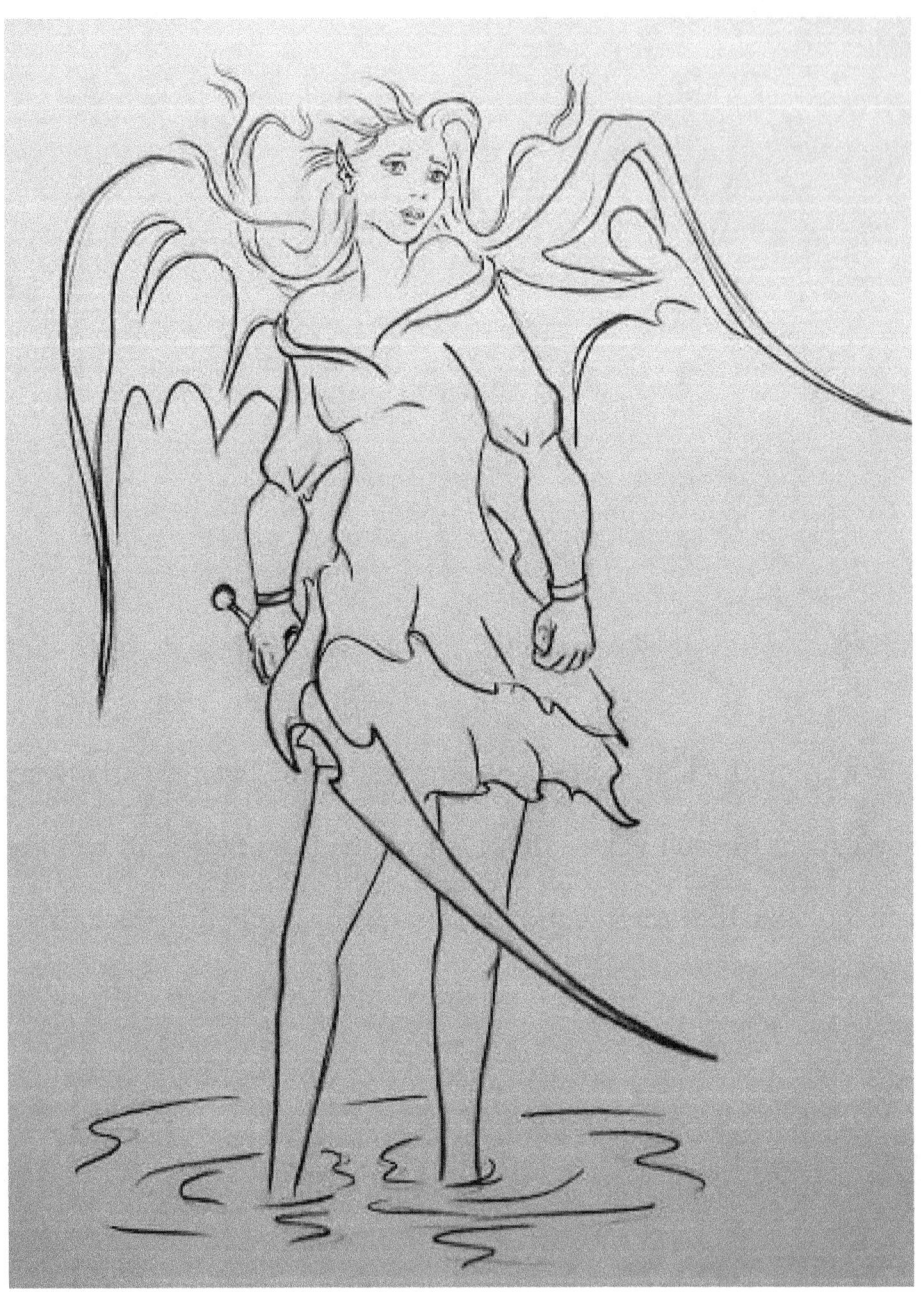

Outline the rest of the body in darker pencil, so that the lines really stand out and you're ready to add detail.

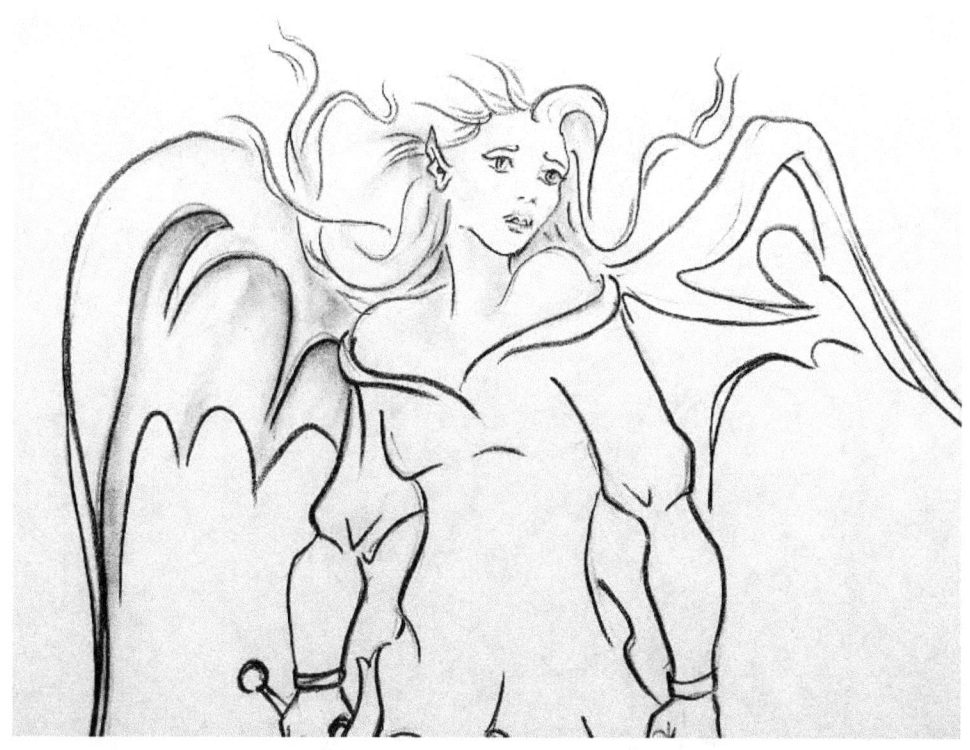

Start shading using the smudging method that we have been going over. Most of the hair is going to be the implication of hair, to give the idea that it is wispy and disappearing.

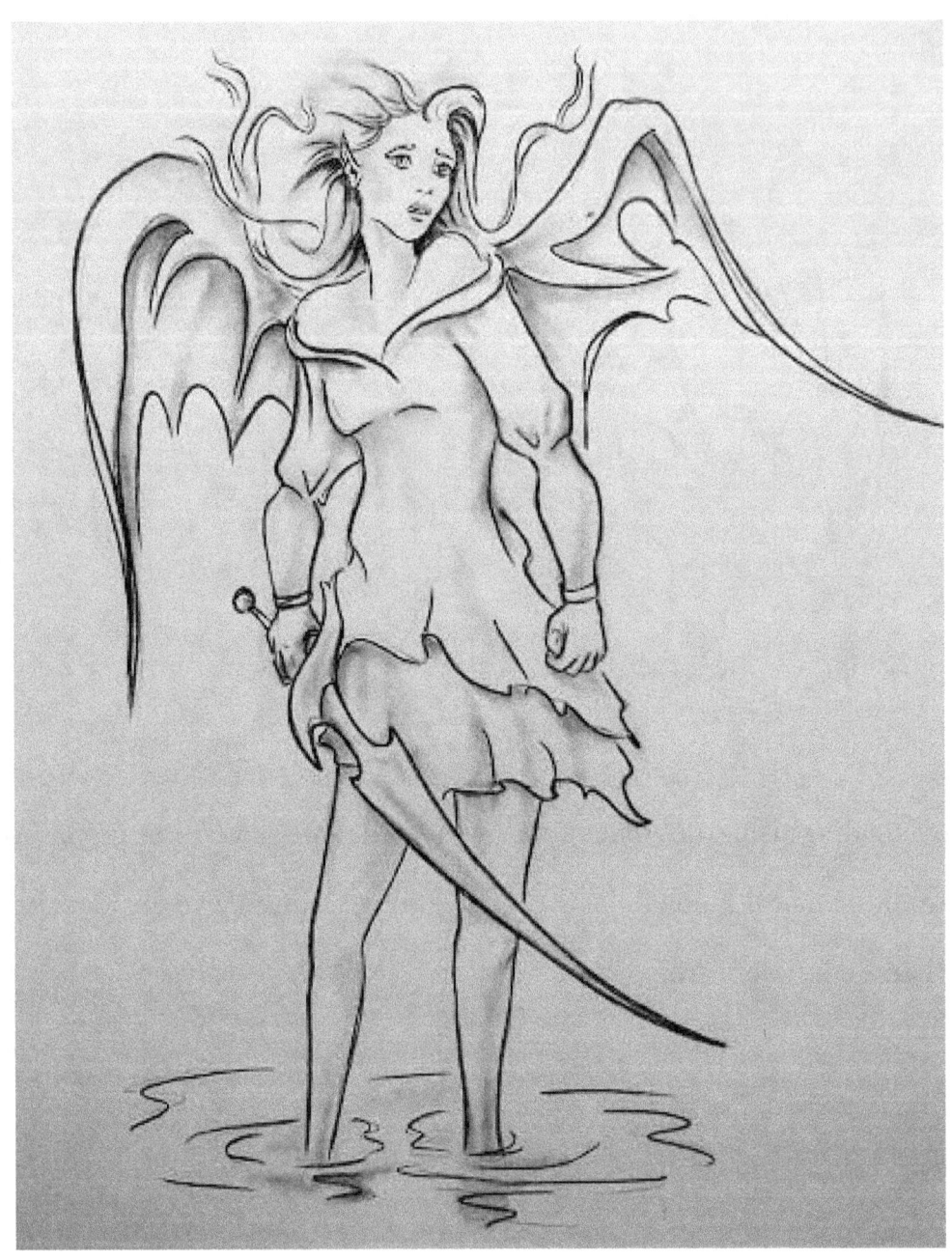

Shade the rest of the body in much the same way. Remember that when it comes to shading the water, you're actually going to be creating the shadow of the Siren.

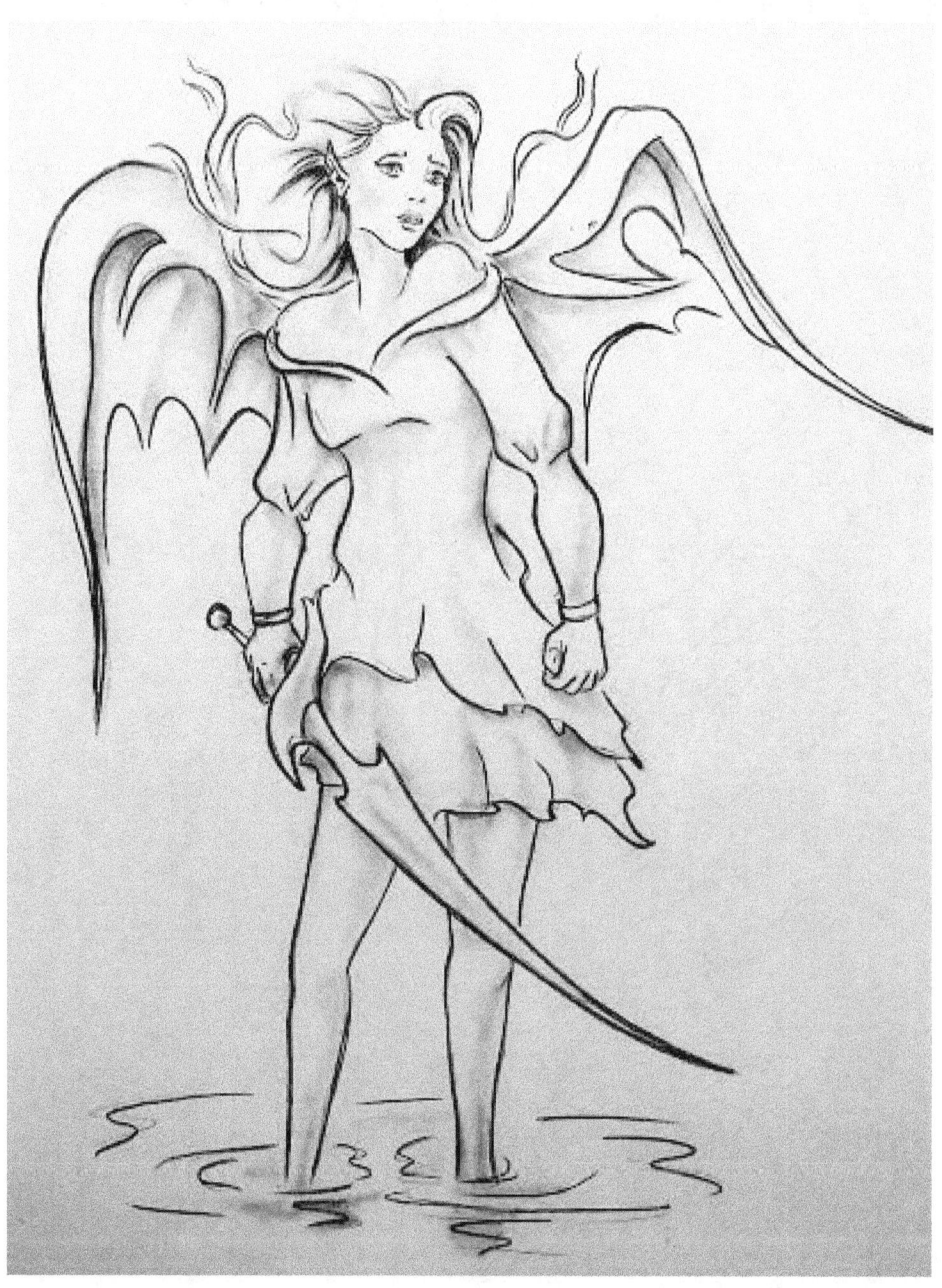

And tada! You have a finished Siren ready to lure your hero to his or her death.

Chapter 4 – Horned Girl

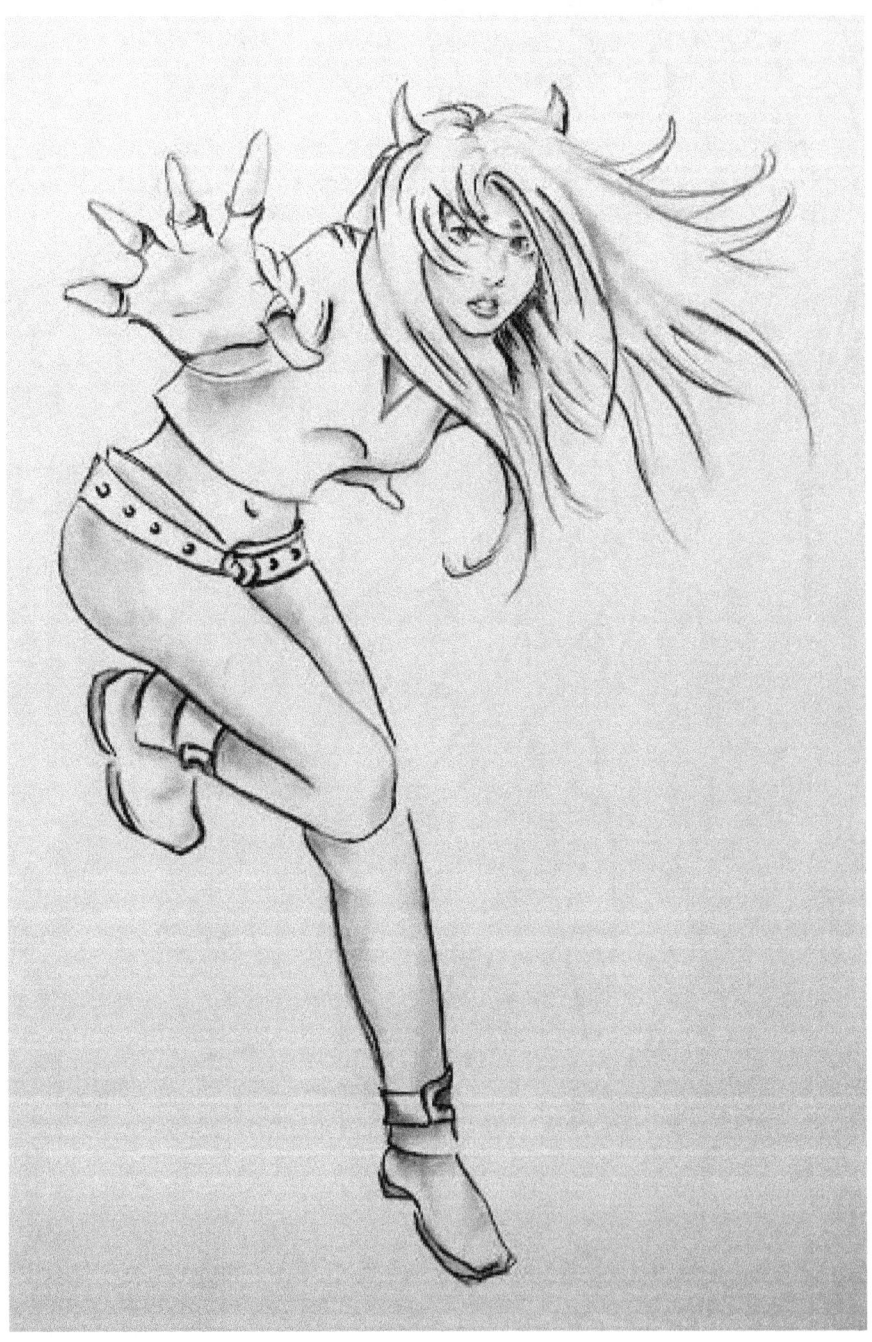

The Horned Girl makes for a great henchmen or ally. She is always ready to fight fiercely for whatever cause that she believes in, and her belief makes her stronger. Here we see an example of foreshortening, or portraying a piece of the work to make it appear three dimensional – in this case, the Horned Girl is reaching forward.

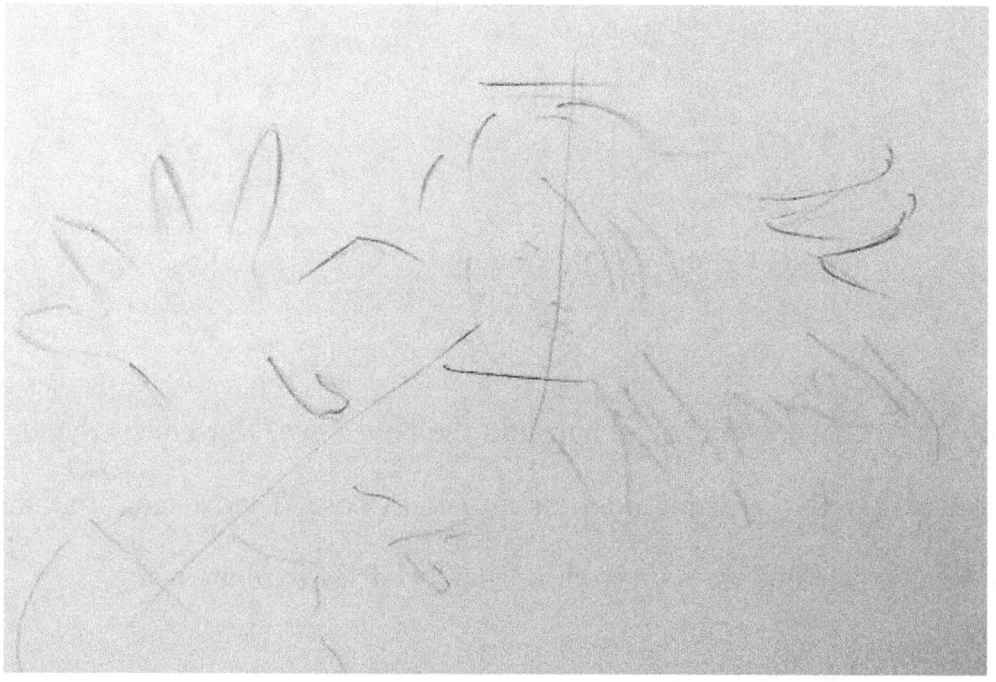

Let's get the outline down. The hand is going to be about the size of the whole head, give or take, so keep that in mind – it's larger because it's supposed to be closer to us. This foreshortening technique is going to hide some of the wrist and most of the arm as well.

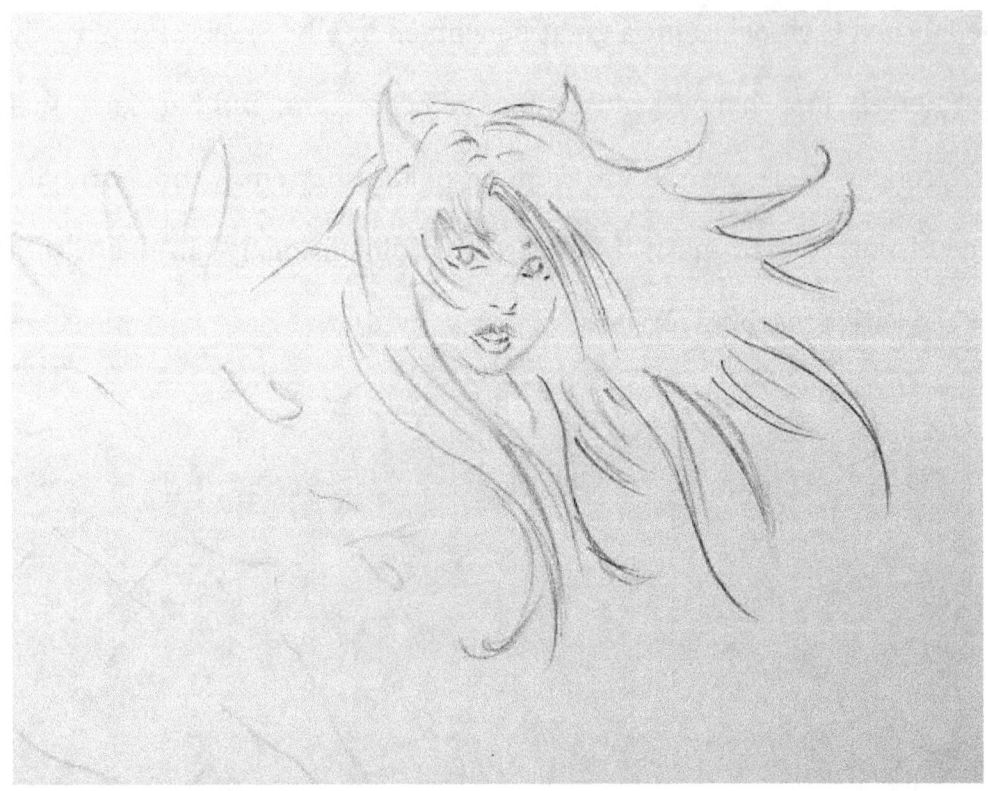

Now let's get the detail of the hair and the face down. Her hair is dynamic, because this is a dynamic pose, or an action pose. That means that she's mid-movement and we want to show that by letting her hair swing.

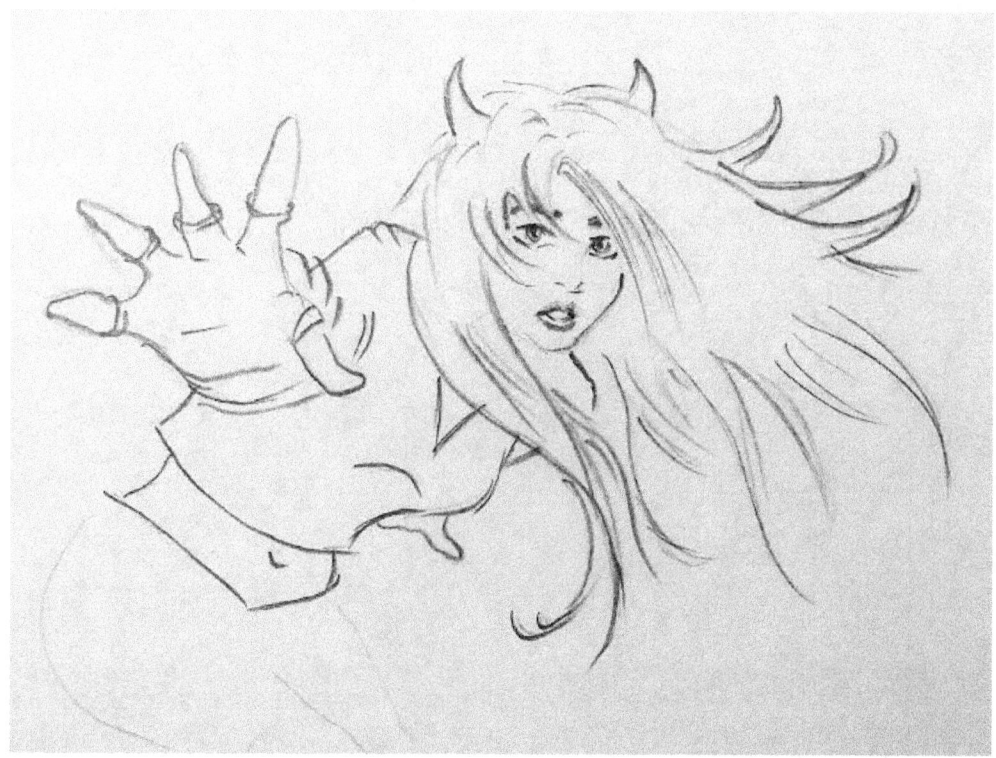

Get the lines of the shirt and the hand in – see how the hand hides the wrist and most of the arm? Also add the pupils to the eyes and the detail to the lips.

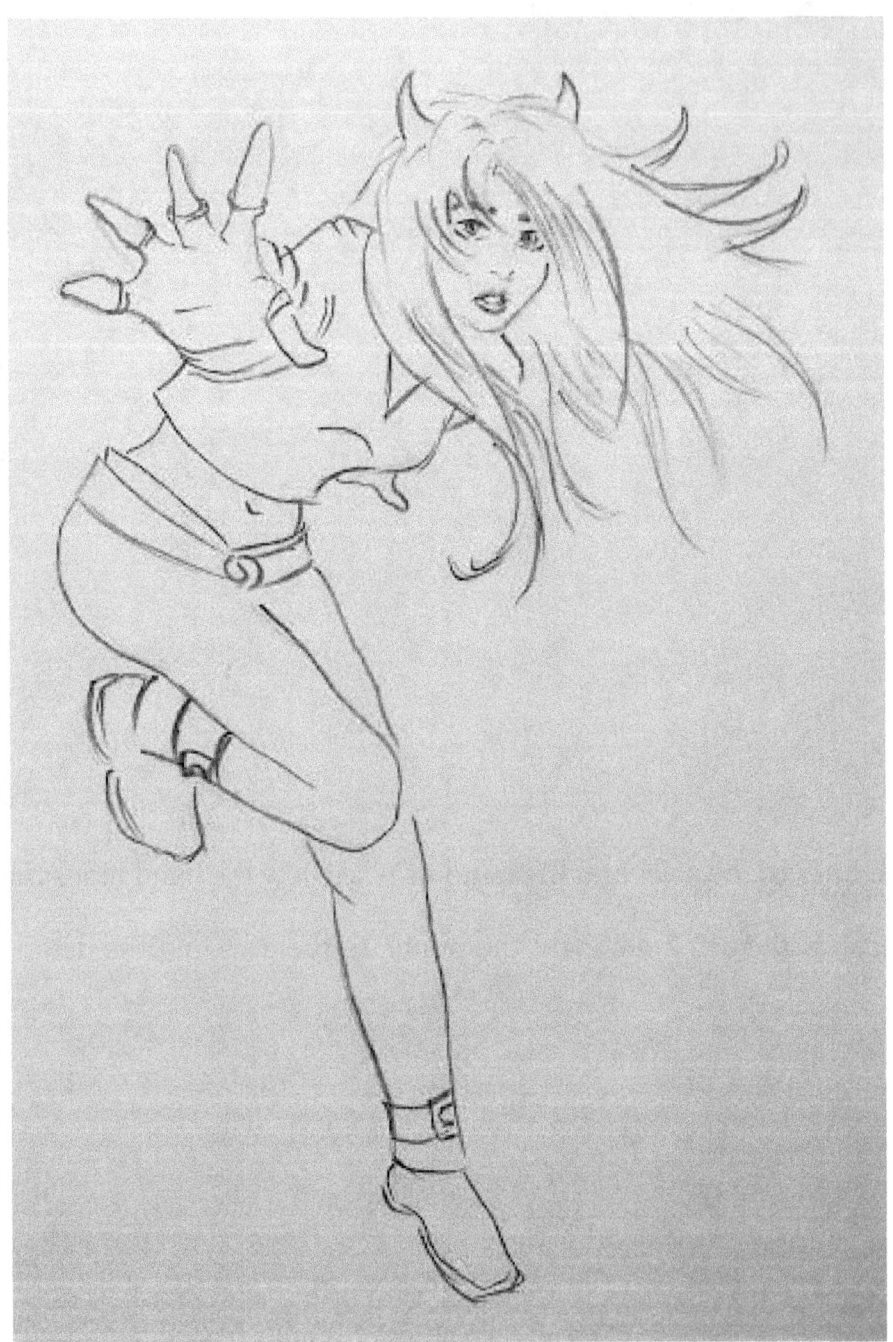

Outline the pants and the feet. Don't be afraid of pressure, we want these lines to stand out.

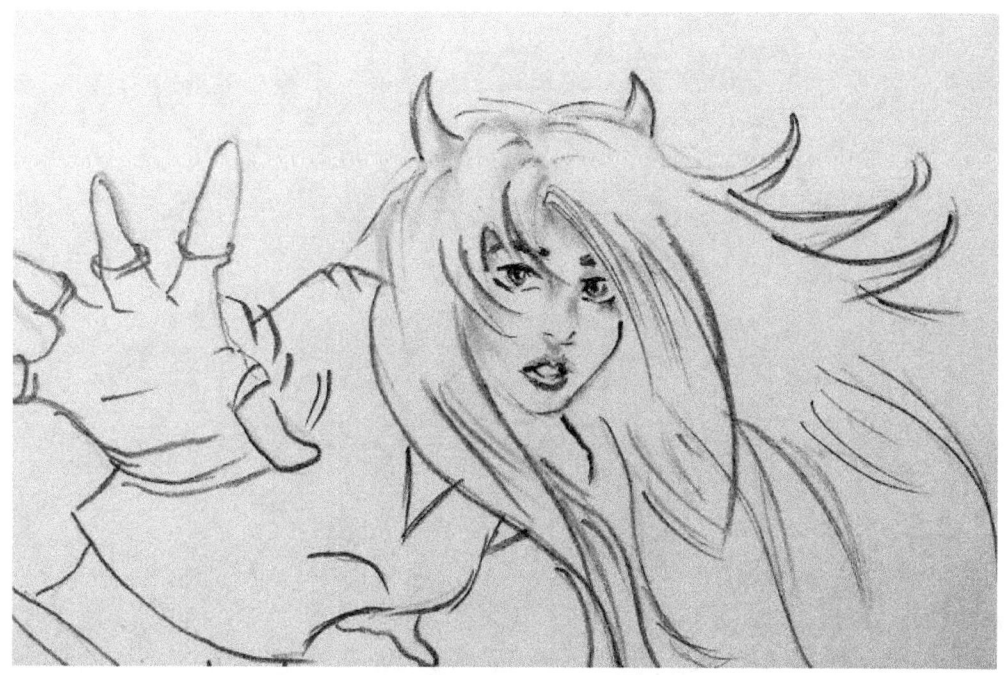

Now we're going to start shading. The hair is going to cast a shadow onto her face, and the horns are going to be shiny and shaded like they're round. We don't want them to look flat – they are three dimensional.

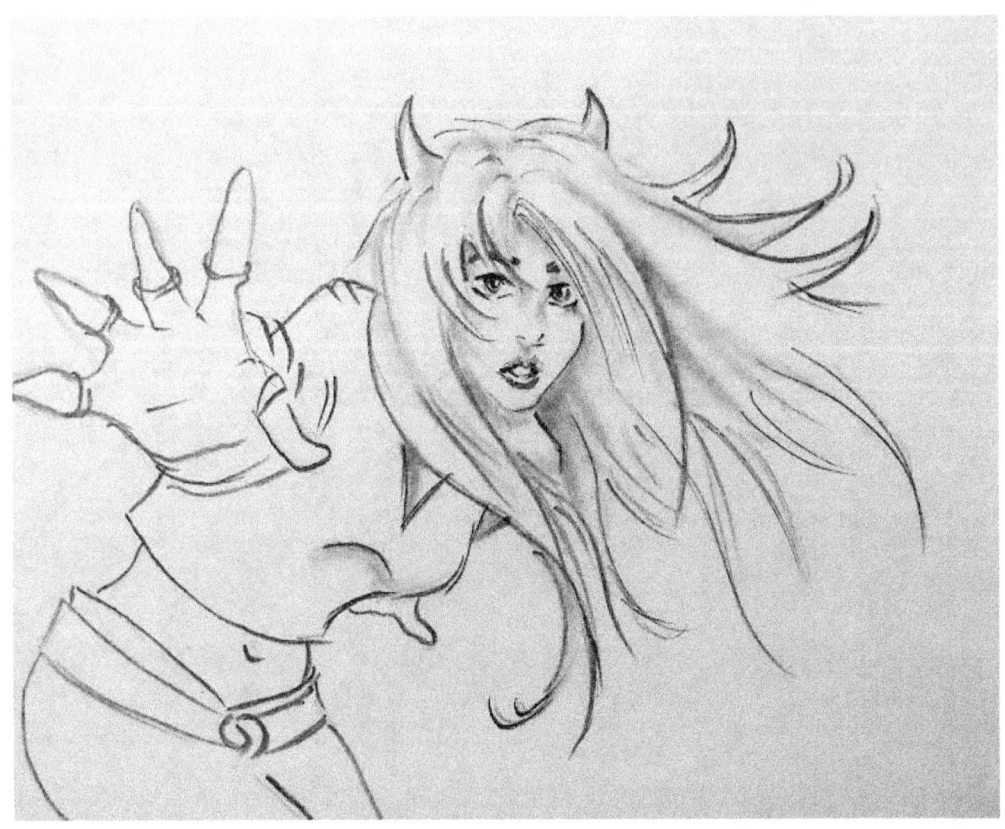

Shade the rest of the hair as well as the curve of the chest, and make sure you shade the face lightly – we don't want to cover up any of the beautiful detail work you just did!

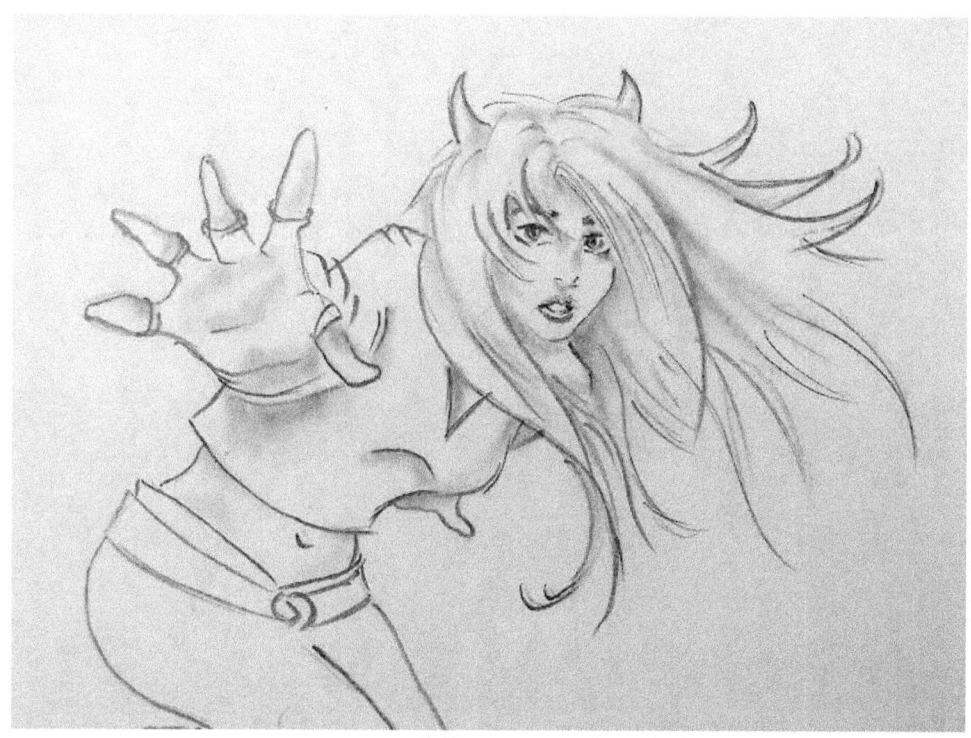

We're going to shade the hand and the rest of the upper body. The hand will be lightly shaded as it is closer to the light source, but it will cast a shadow onto the Horned Girl's side. This shadow is going to be kind of dark, because arms are dense.

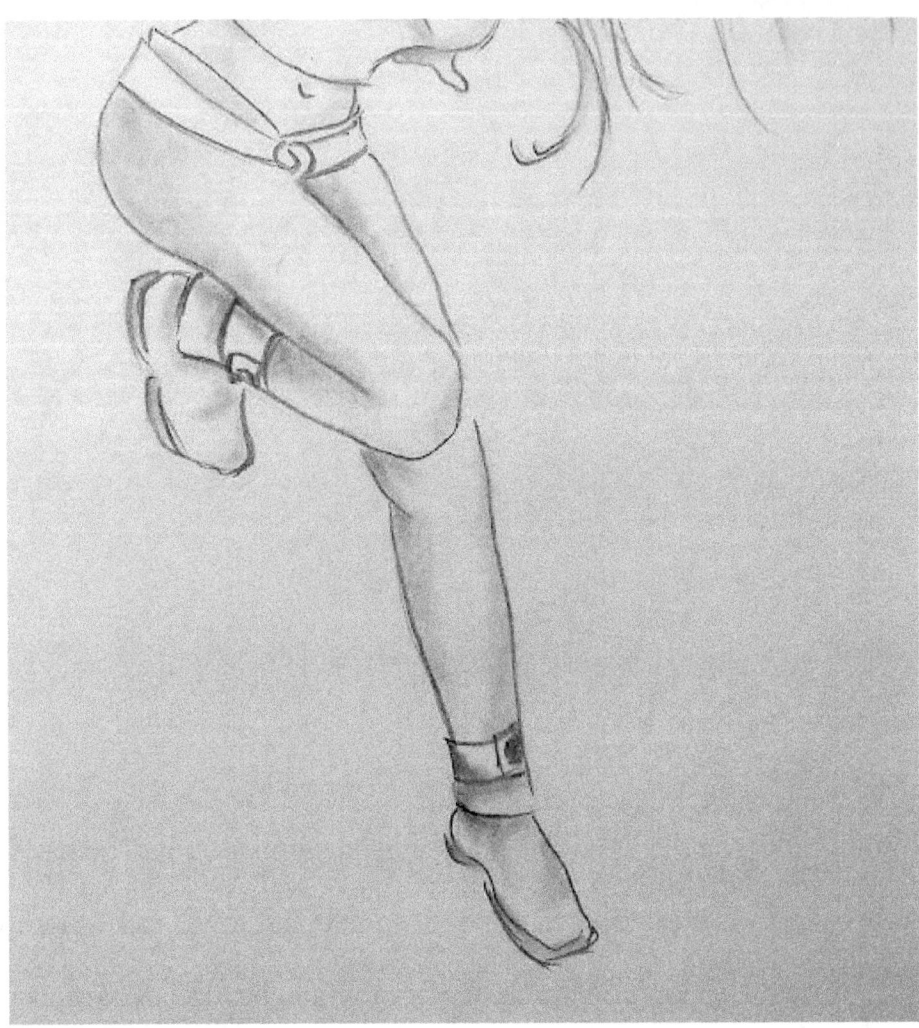

Next, shade the lower body, using the same smudging technique. Notice that the pants are getting more shade than the shirt – this is because we're also giving it a shade of grey that indicates it's a darker color than the shirt.

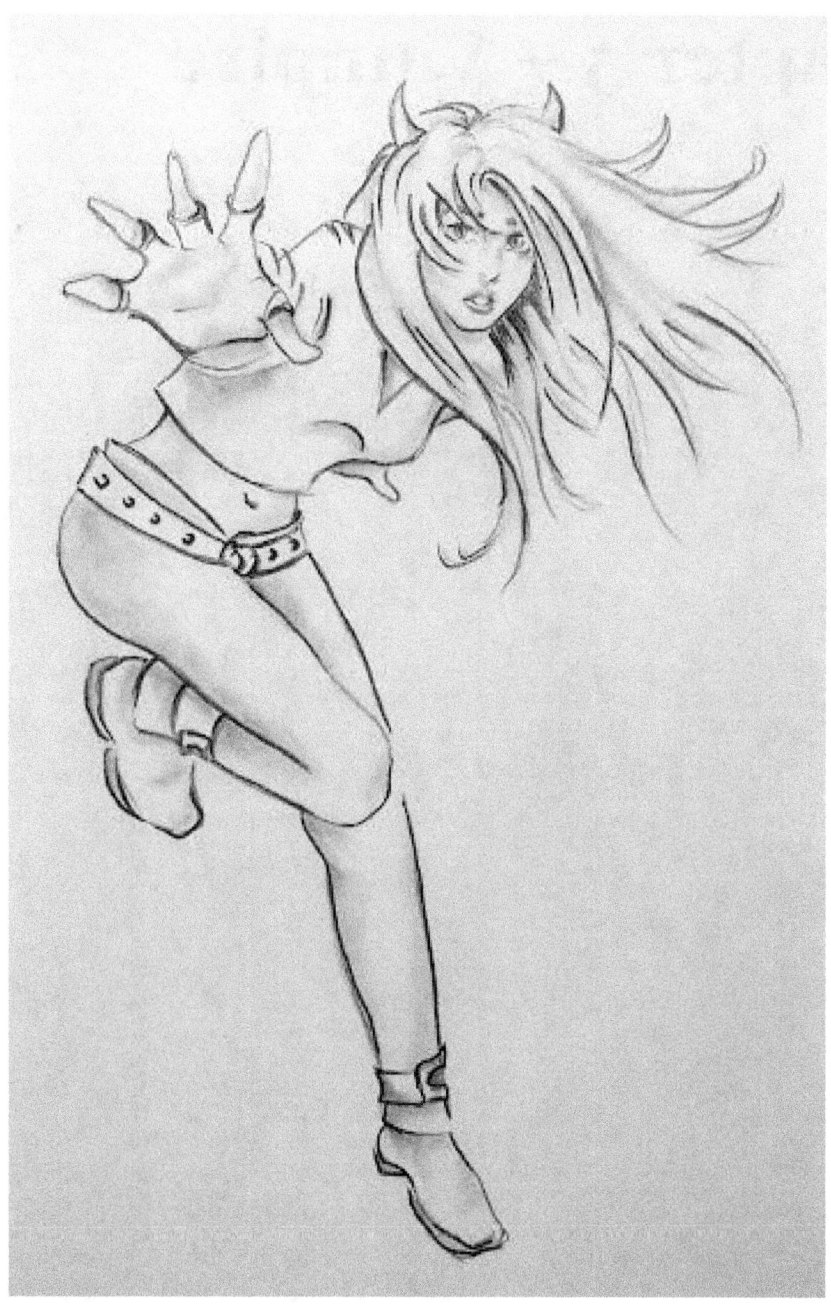

Finalize the lines and voila! You're done! You now have a Horned Girl ready to fight for everything that she believes to be true and right.

Chapter 5 – Vampire

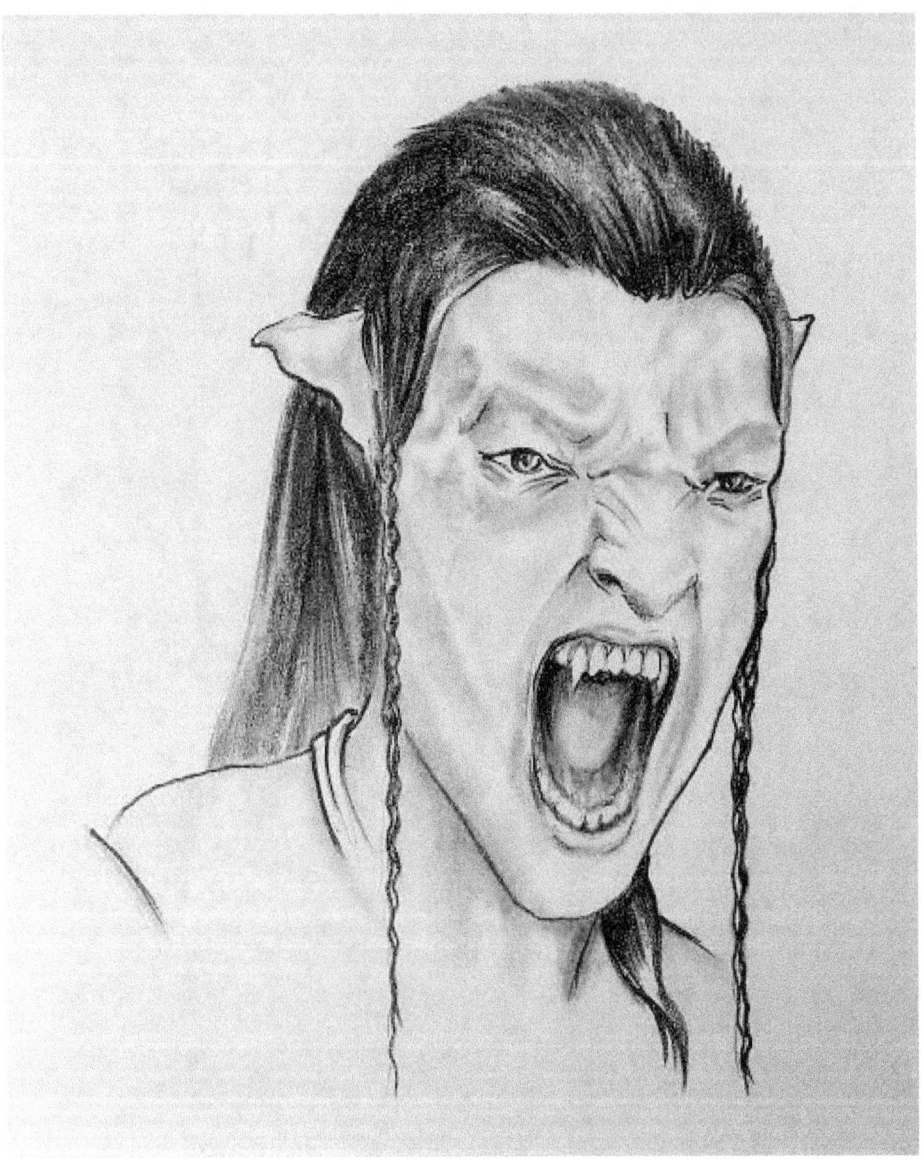

The Vampire is a bloodthirsty villain, perfect to threaten your hero or

heroine with sharp fangs and sweet words. The Vampire is a classic fantasy creature, one that is a lot of fun to draw and a lot of fun to work into your comic or story.

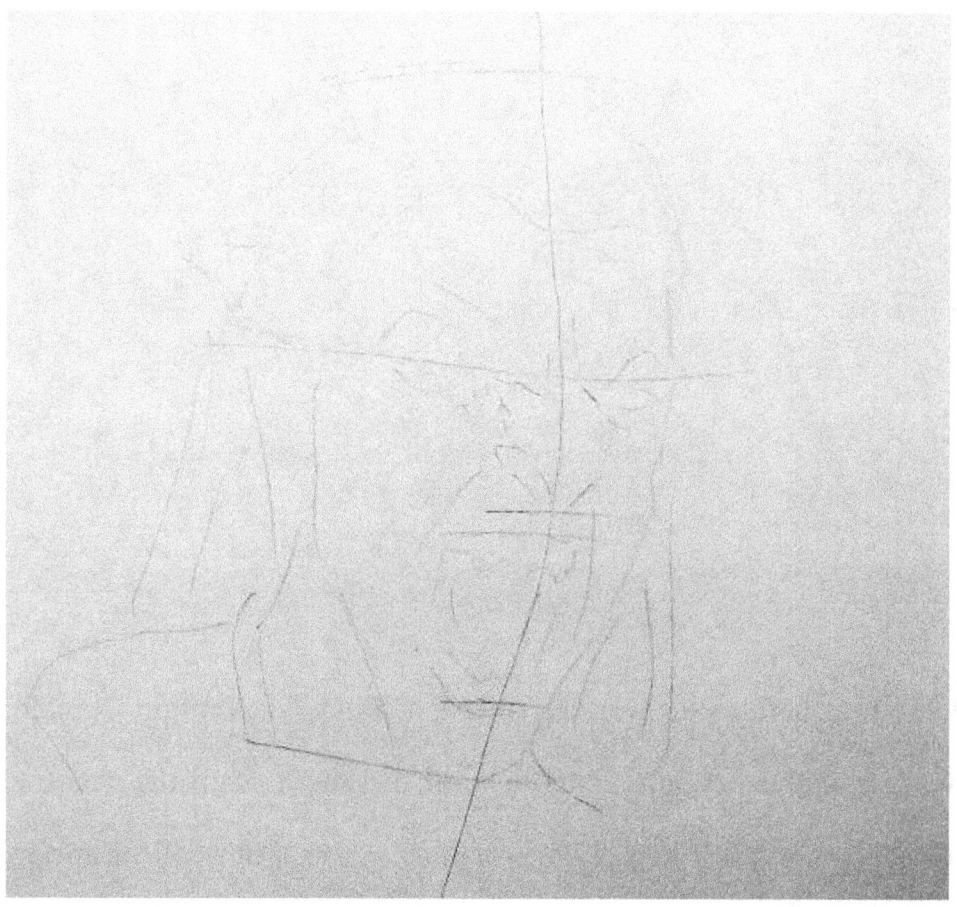

First block out the areas where the features of the vampire will be. It's okay if it looks square here, we'll smooth it out later. Right now we want to get the basic areas down.

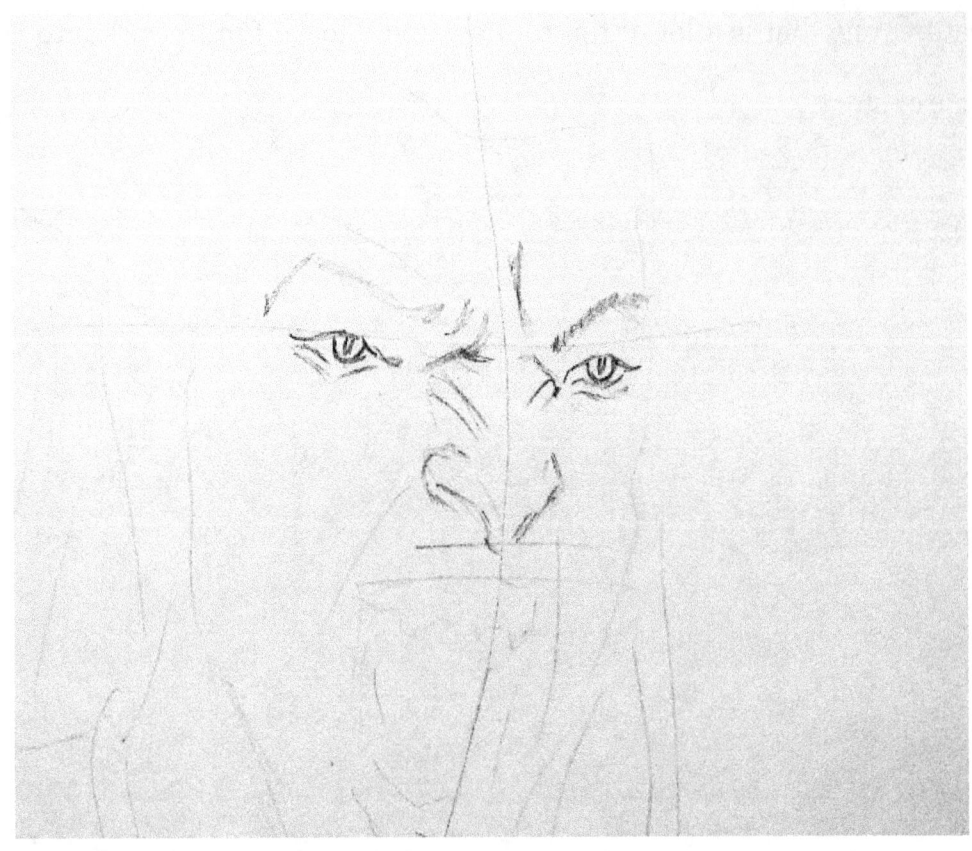

Now we're going to start working on the details. This Vampire is making a very aggressive expression, and we want to show that in the way that he wrinkles his nose. If it helps, make the face yourself in a mirror and take a look at how your own nose wrinkles.

His eyes are slits as well, which is different than the eyes we have done before. This Vampire is otherworldly.

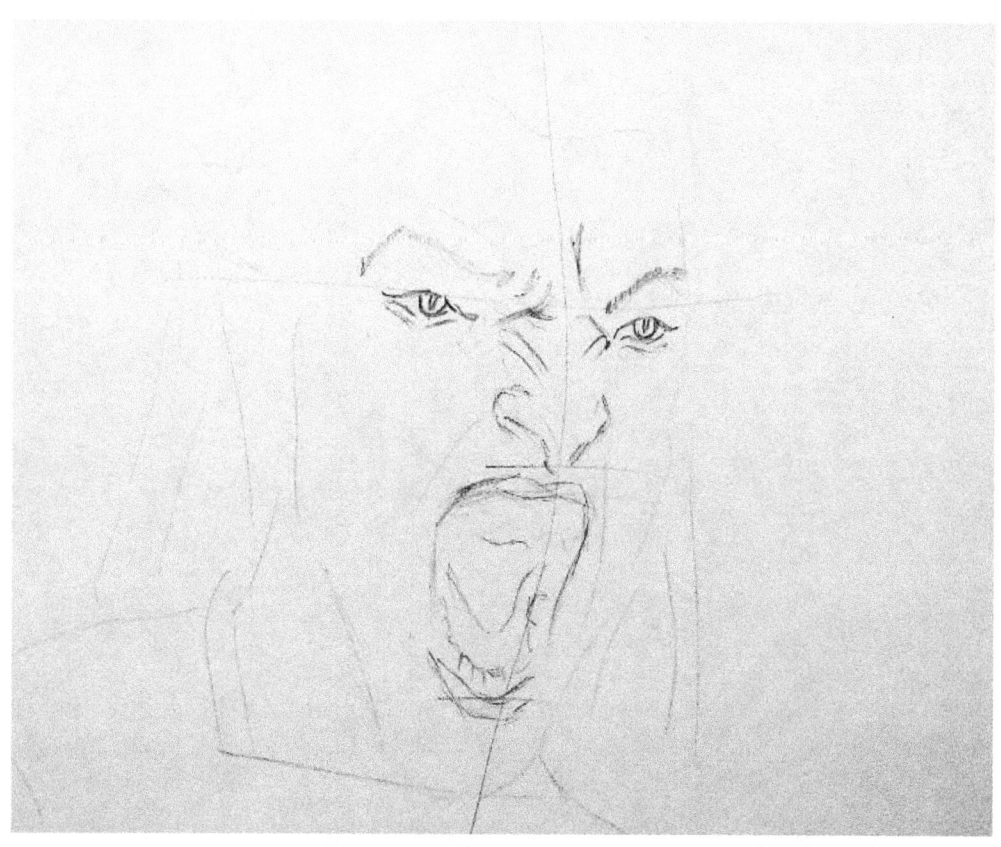

The details of the mouth are a little complicated. We want to get the basic outline of the teeth and tongue, as well as the lips. The snarl is going to hide a lot of the upper lip.

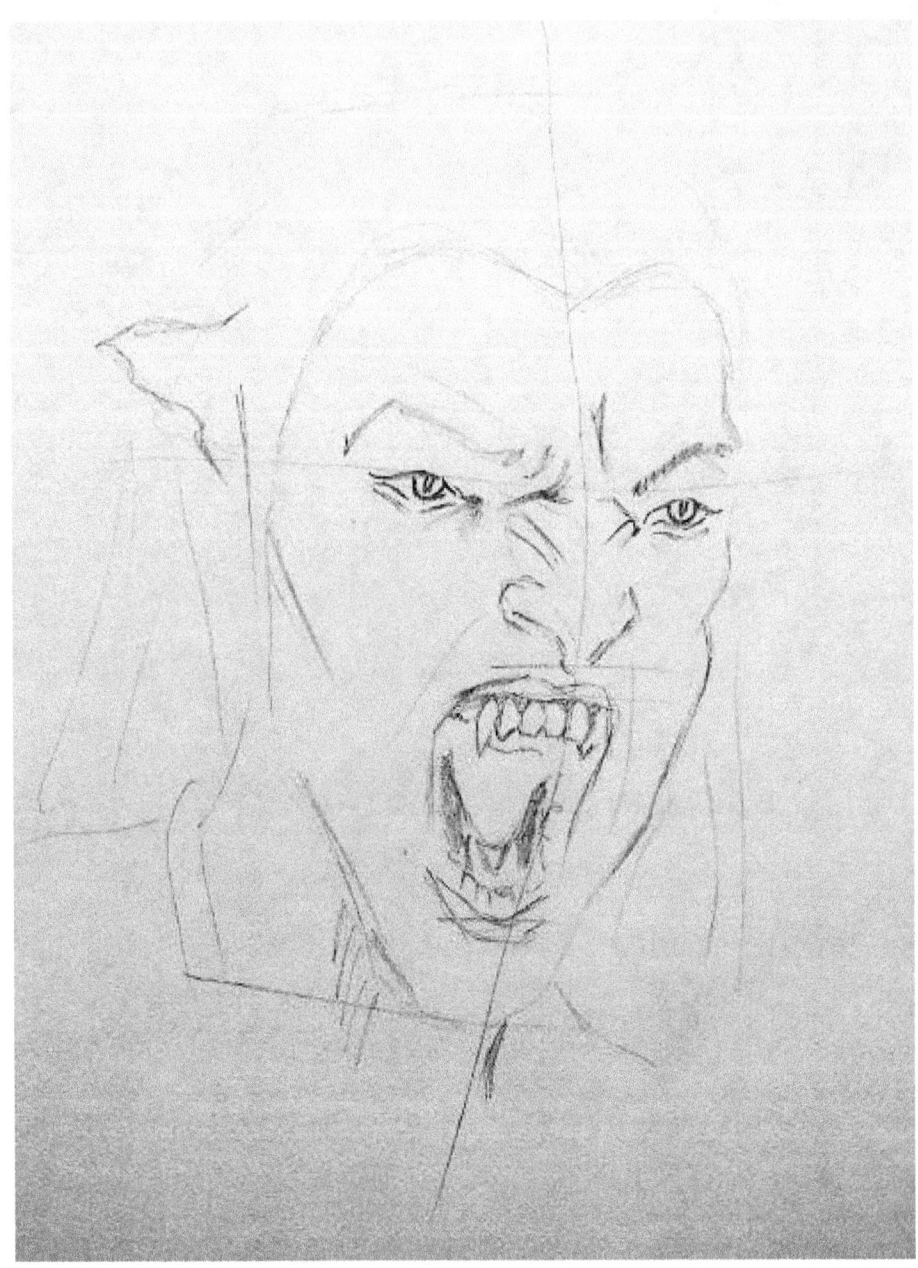

Finalize the mouth detail by drawing in the teeth and fangs – the Vampire is ready to lunge at any exposed neck that it can.

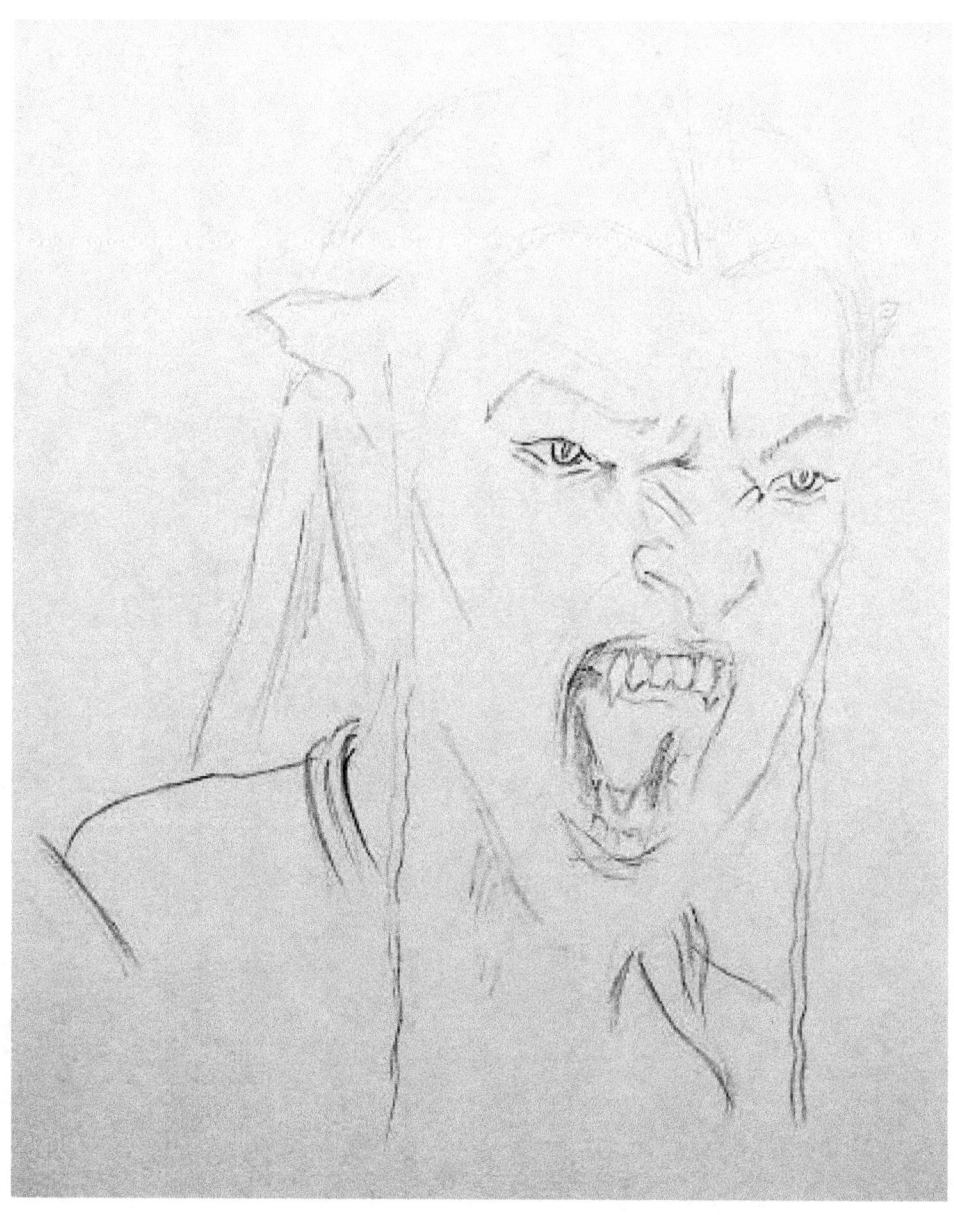

Add the lines in for the hair and the ear, and begin working on the neck and shoulders.

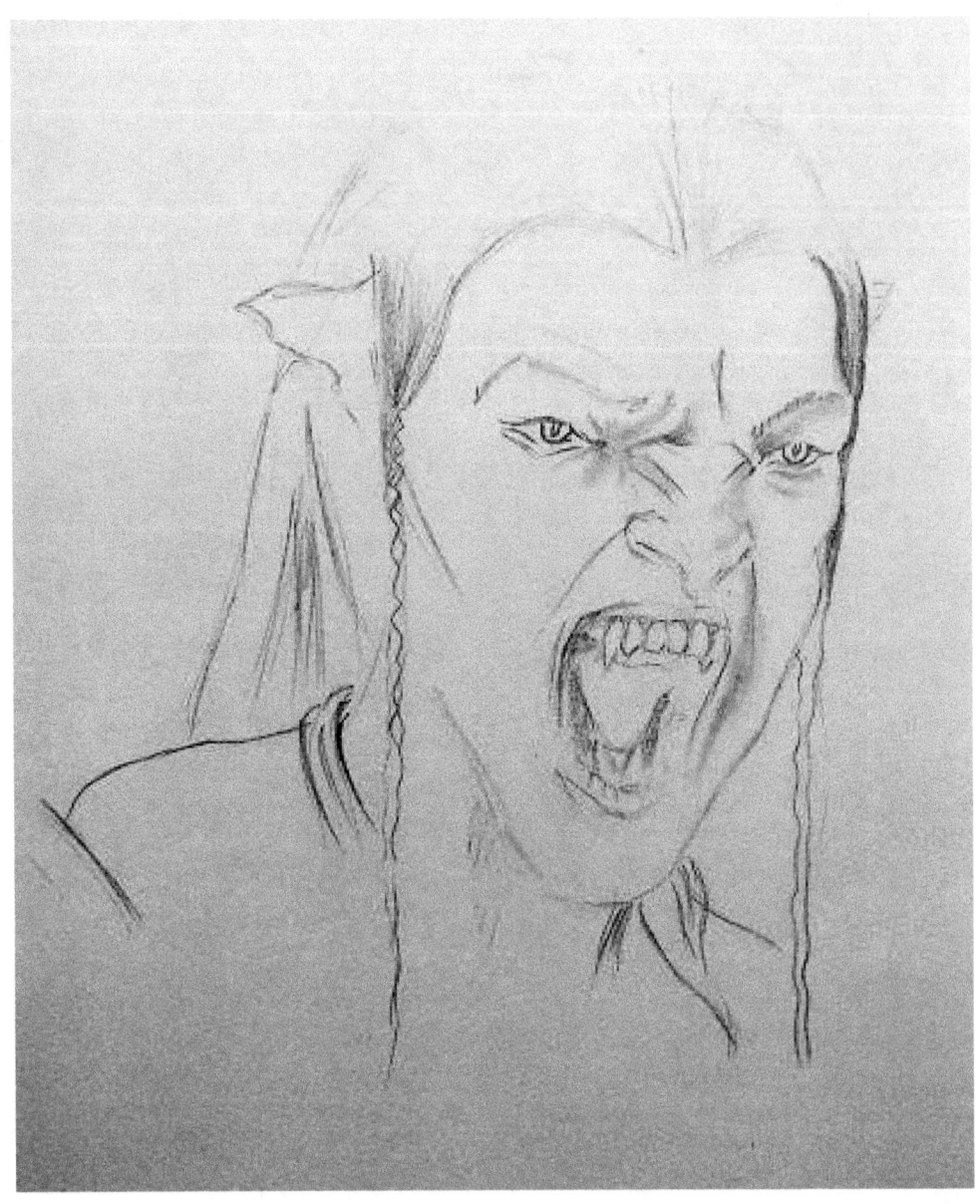

Now we're going to start shading the face and some of the hair. Remember the smudging technique we've been learning. For the hair, use lots of lines bunched together to give the illusion of strands making up the bunch of hair.

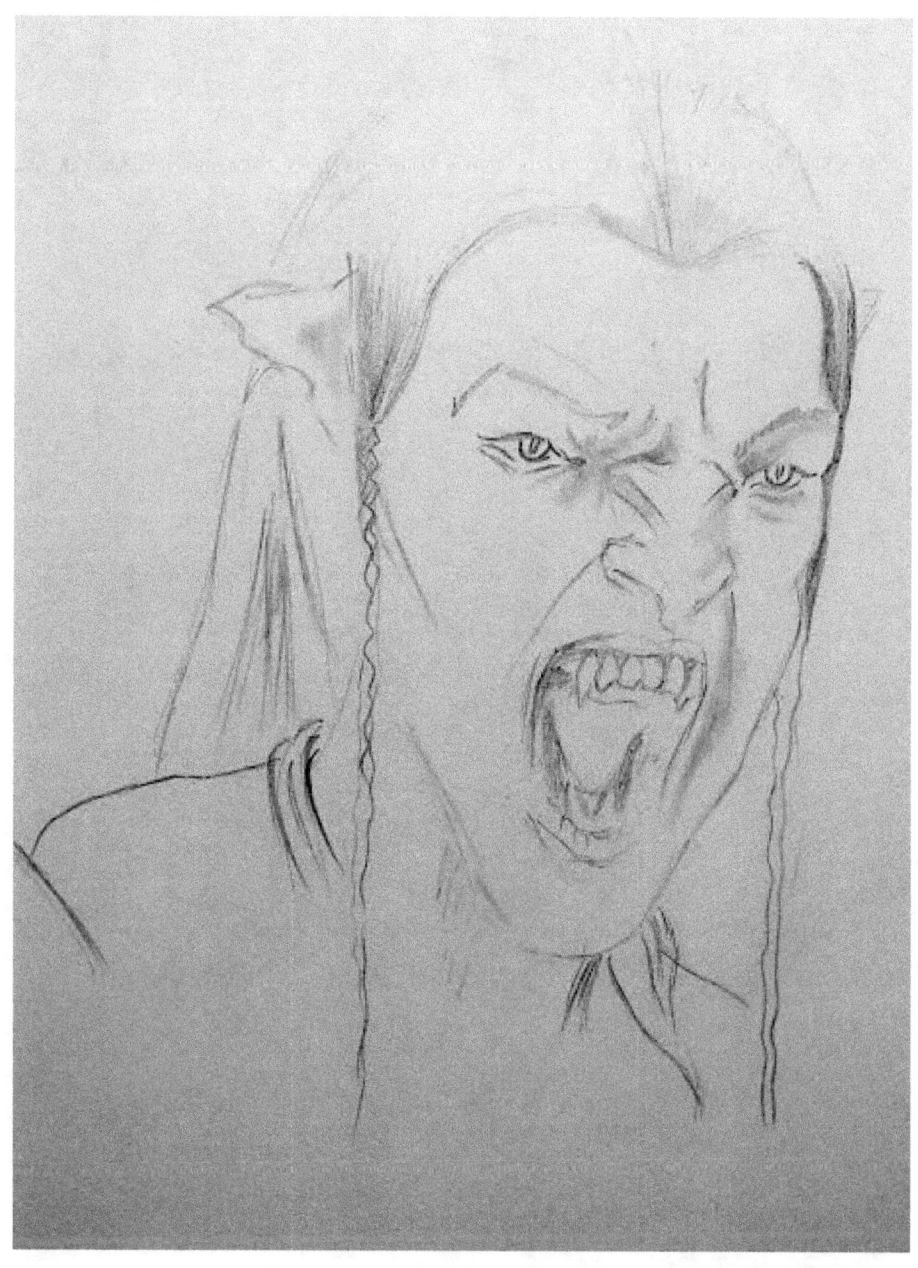

Continue to shade the ear and the rest of the hair, as well as a little bit on the neck.

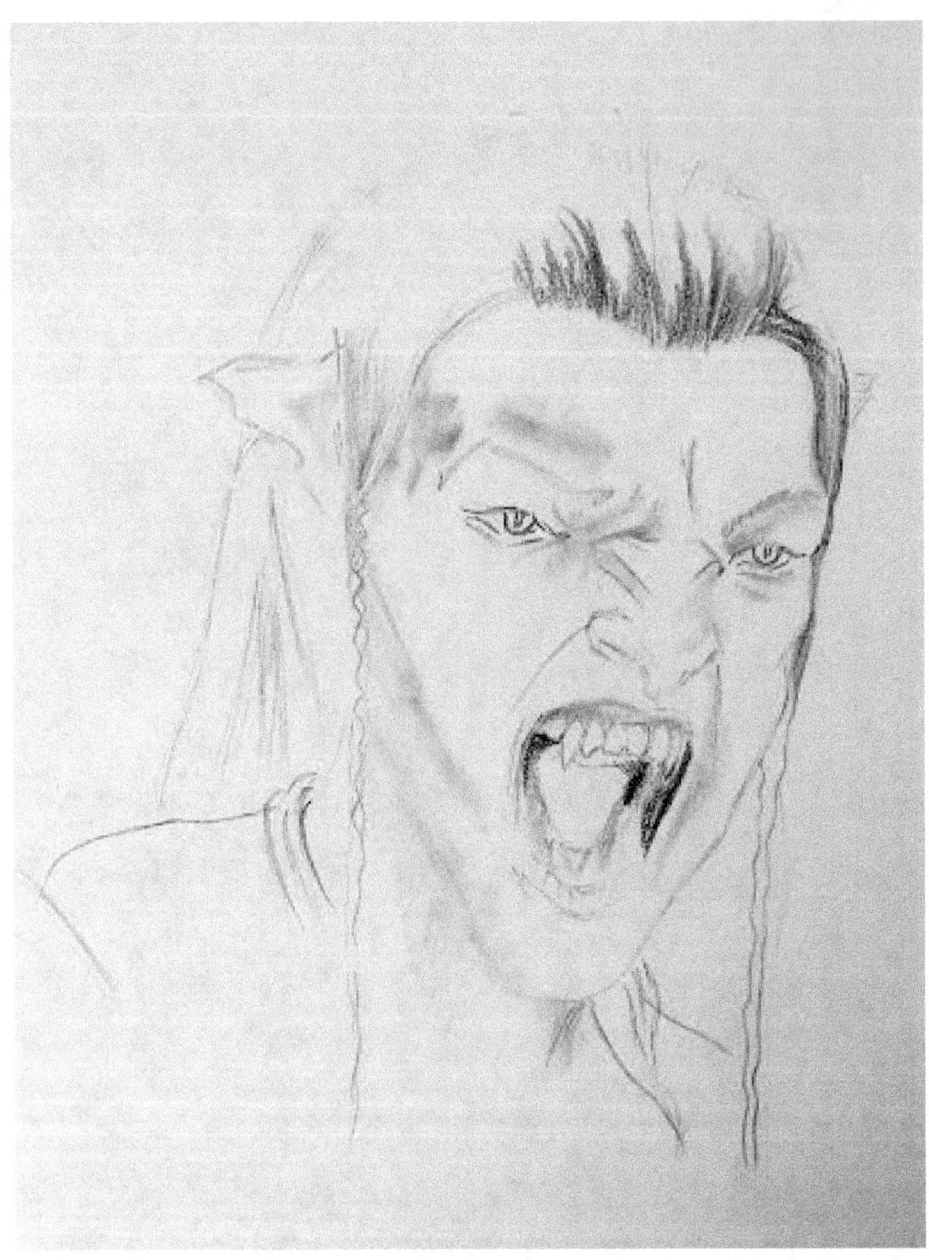

Shade the jaw line – our Vampire is creepy and we want him to look his scariest. Shading is a great way to do that, as the darker or more detailed a villain is, the scarier they are.

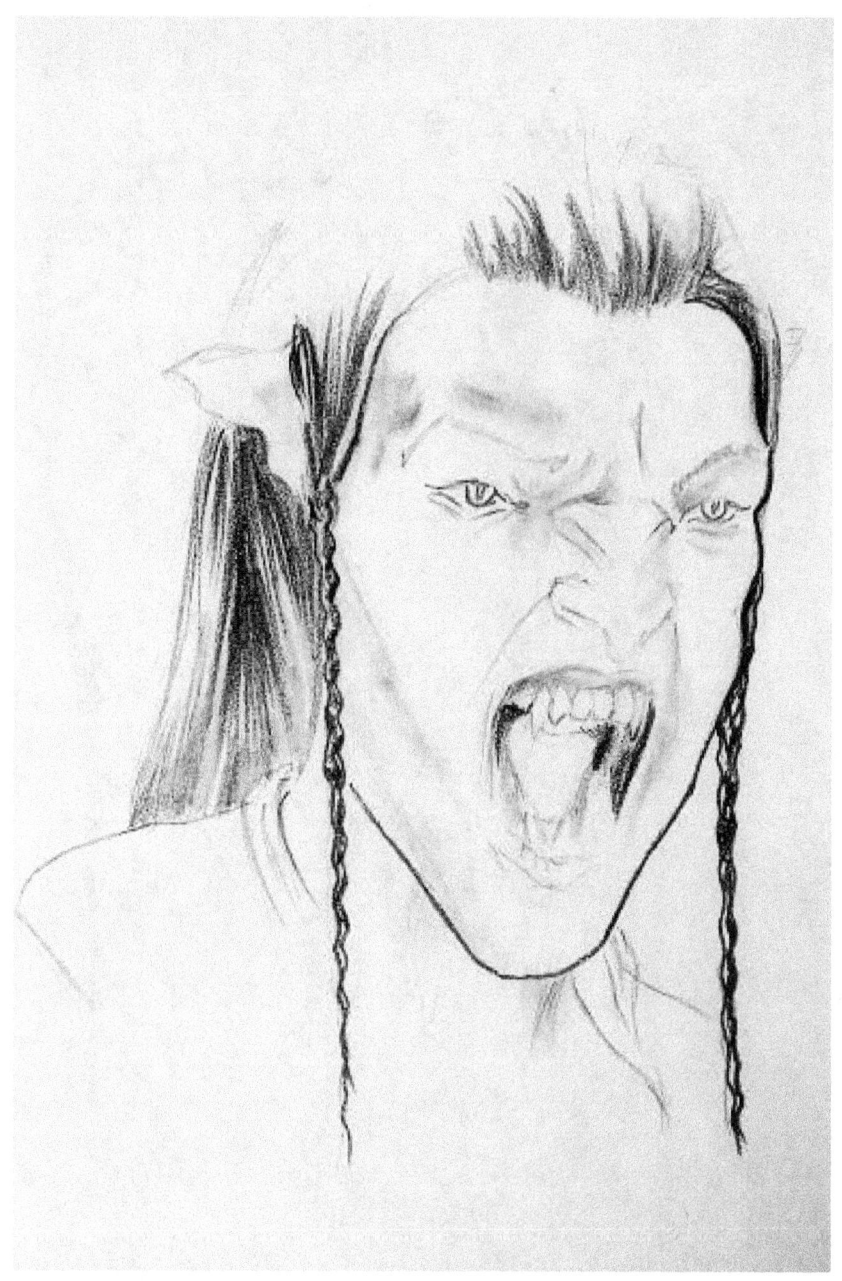

Keep shading the hair. We want to give the idea that the hair is a very dark color, so don't be afraid of pressure here. The darker the better.

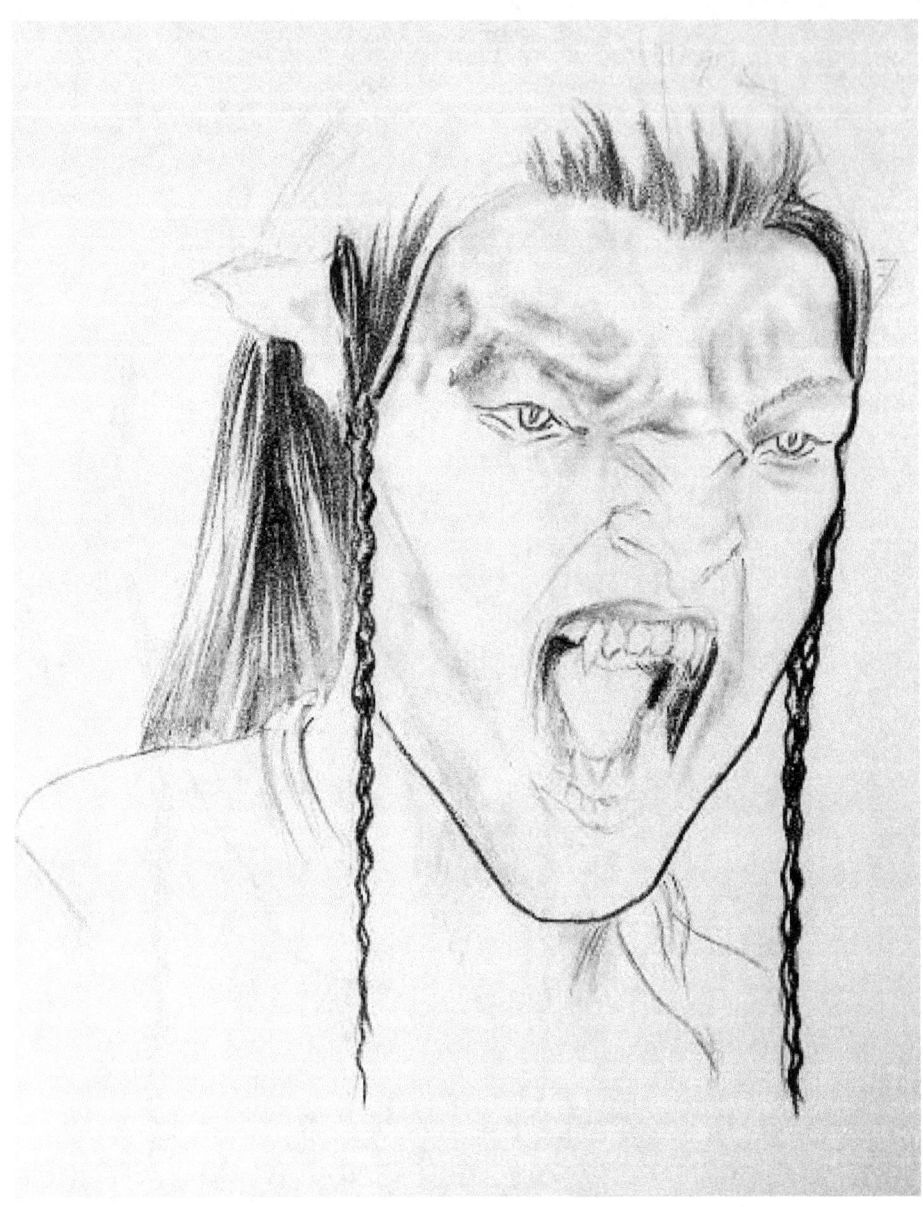

The wrinkles on the Vampire's forehead can be difficult, but be patient. Remember you can also use the eraser technique – smudge and then erase the places you need to be shiny or free of smudges.

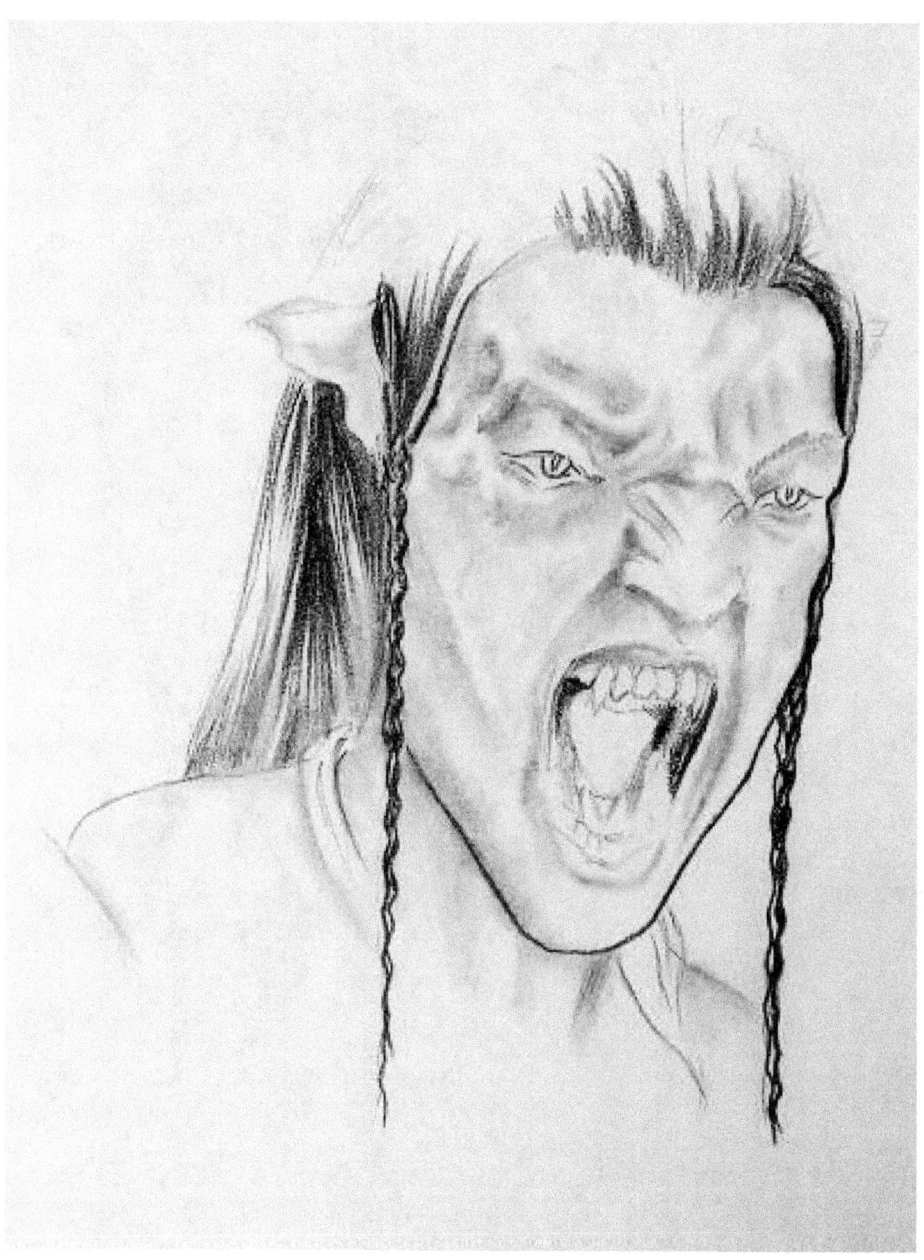

Now do the shading around the Vampire's cheeks with the same smudge and erase technique.

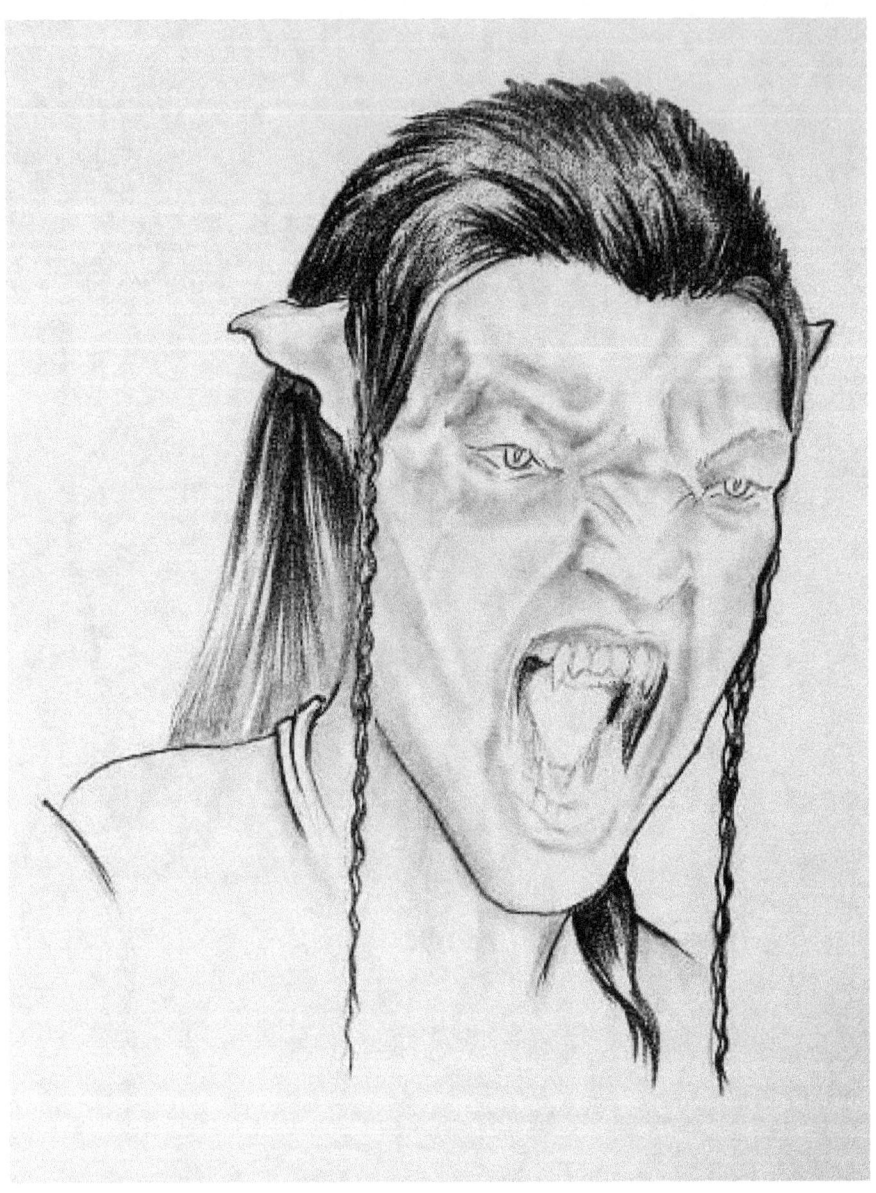

Add in more of the hair, using sweeping, dark strokes of your pencil. You can also use the eraser technique, but be very precise and careful as you do.

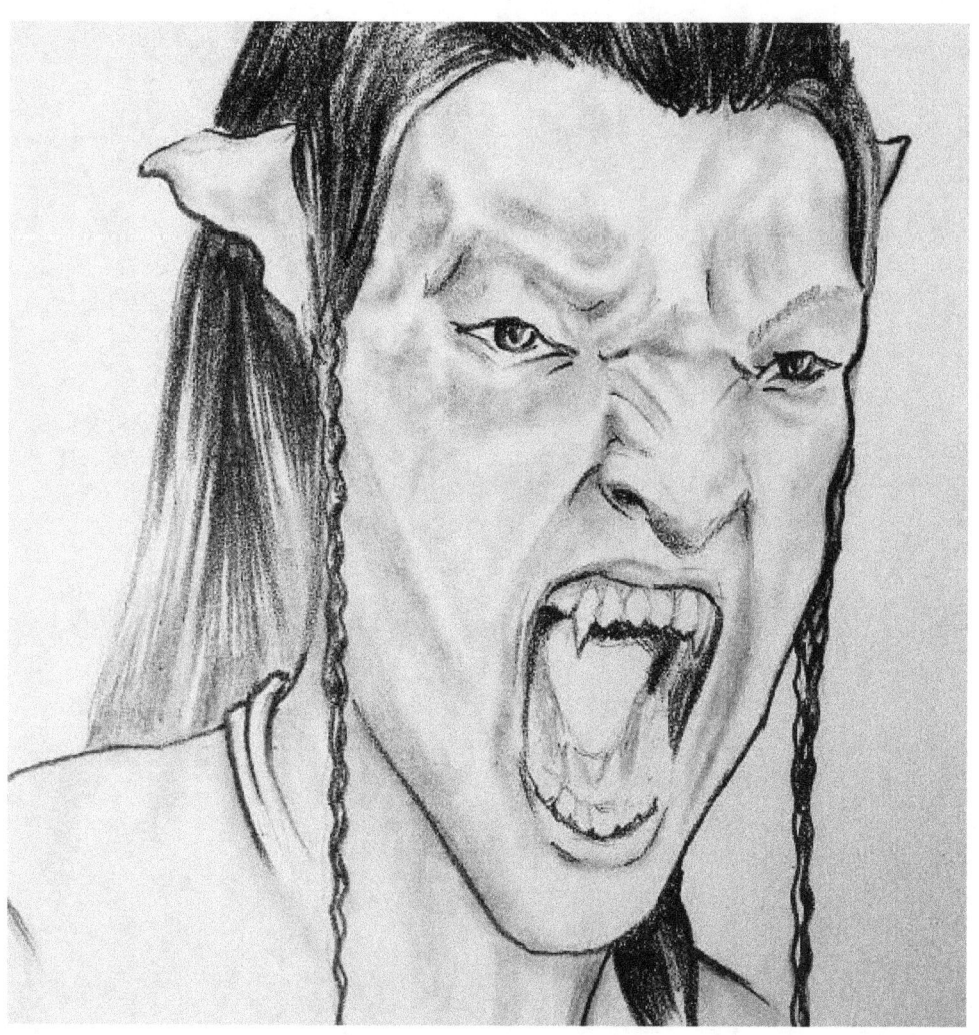

Now we're going to add in some details to the eyes and nose. Darken the lines that you want to stand out, really give our Vampire some texture and some striking features.

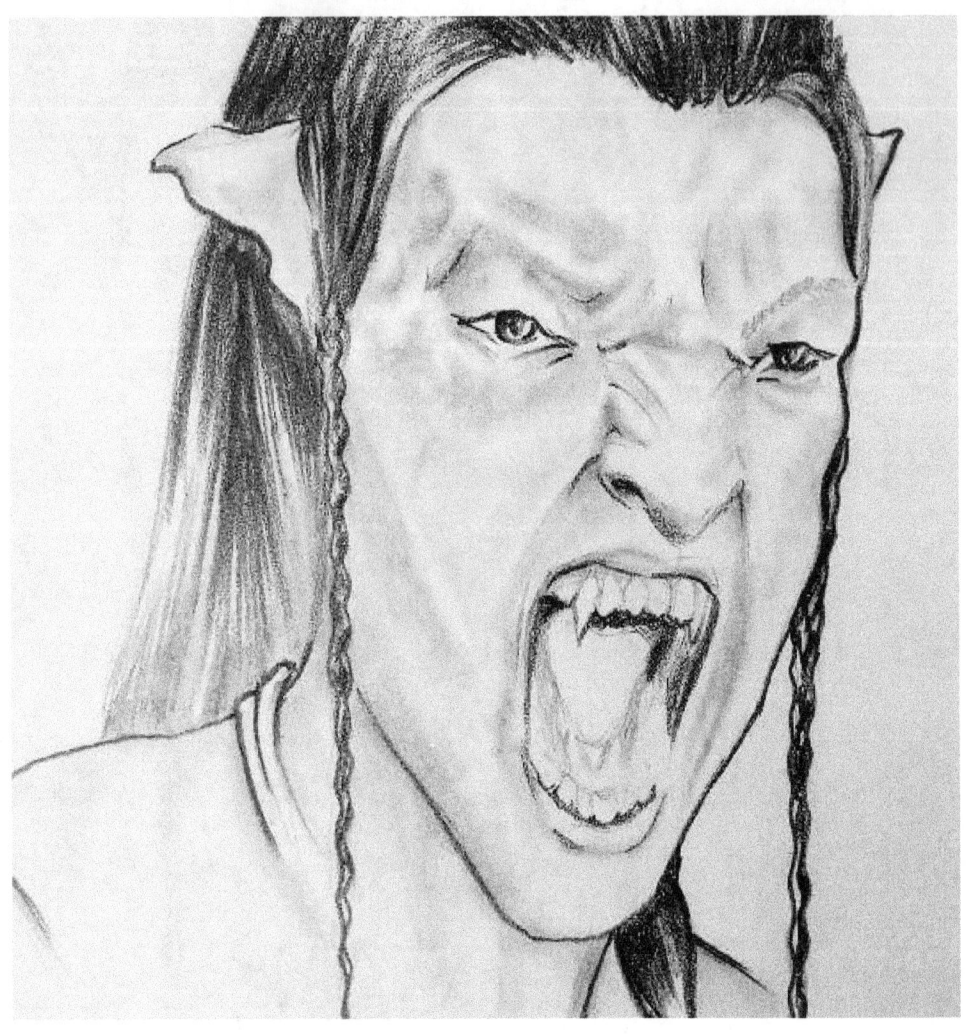

Keep adding detail, smudge them a little to smooth them as you go.

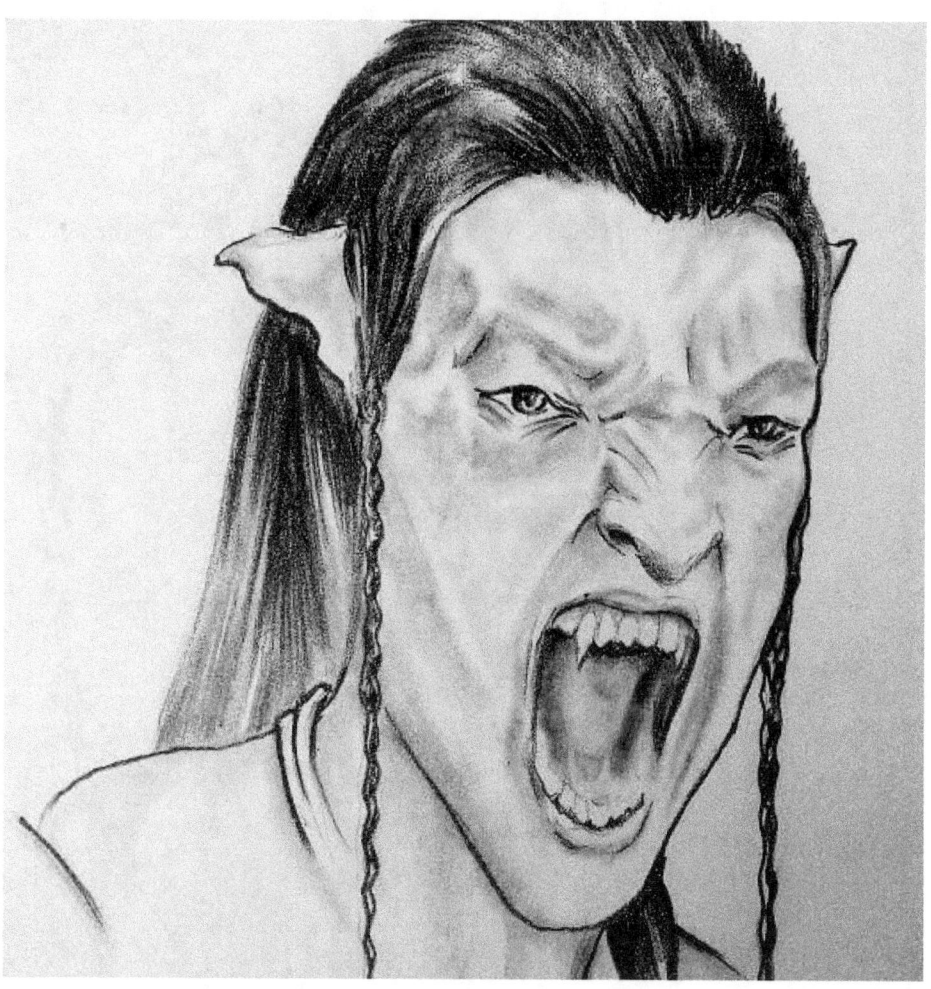

For the tongue, smudge it into the teeth a little, giving the idea that he is hissing or somehow moving it.

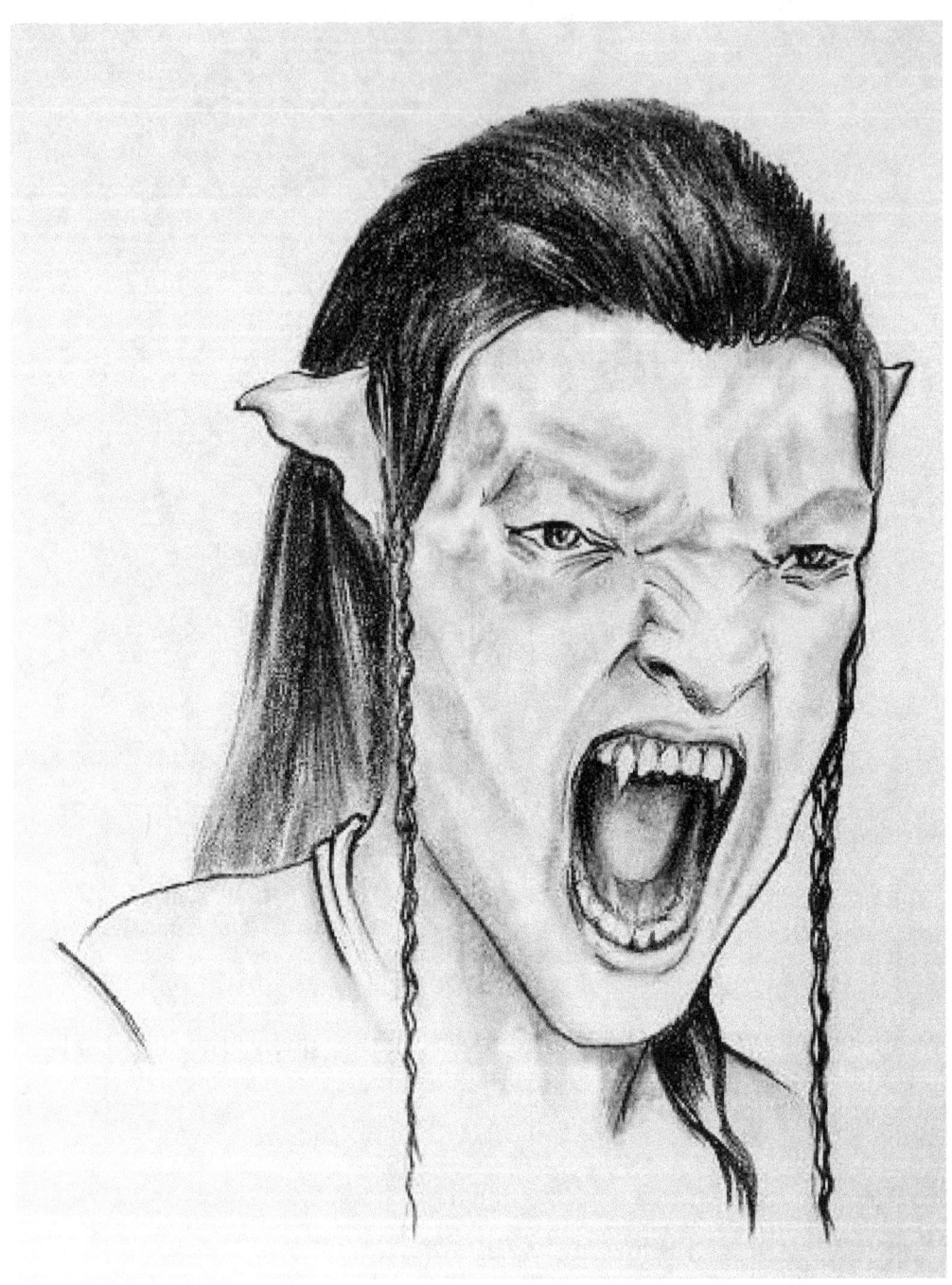

And there is your finished Vampire, ready to scare your hero or heroine!

Your Vampire is ready to start sucking blood at any time.

Chapter 6 – Snake Shifter

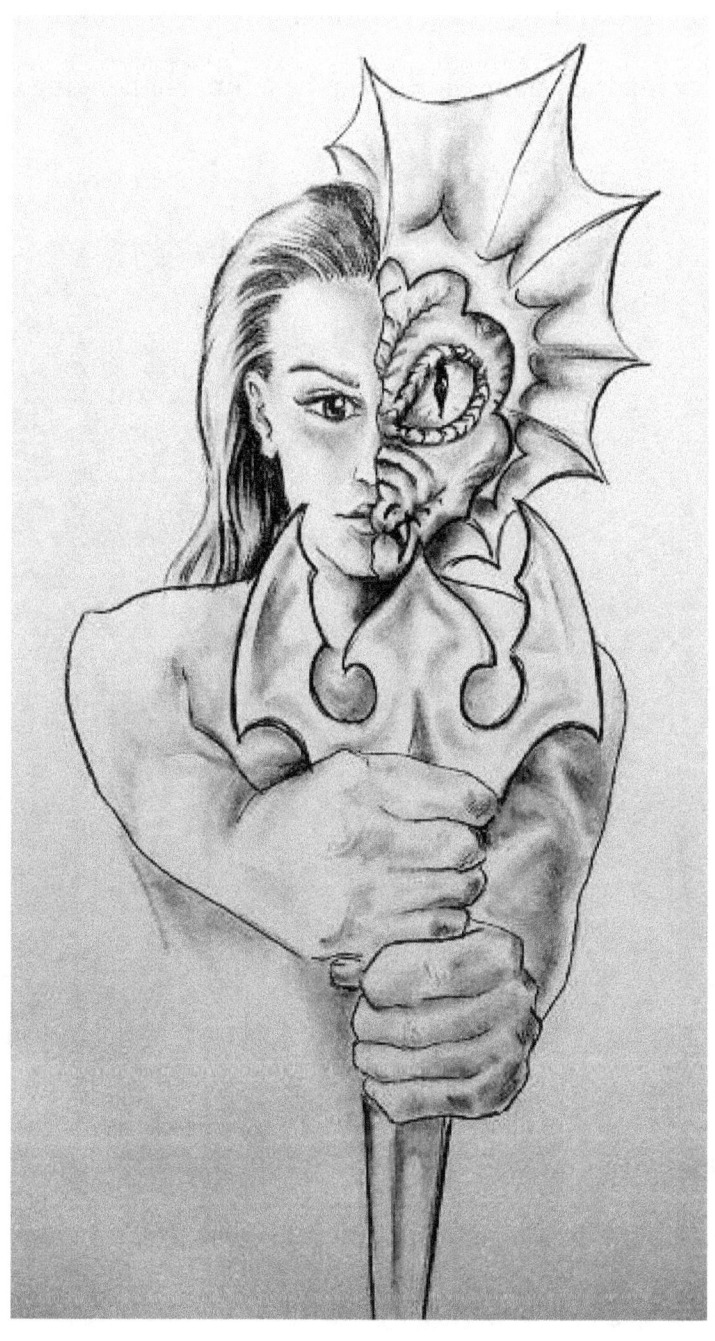

Part of the Snake Shifter's prowess in battle comes from her ability to shift into a snake at will. Imagine a half-snake woman coming towards you across a field of your brethren fighting for their lives – it would be completely terrifying. Drawing the Snake Shifter can be a fun, challenging experience.

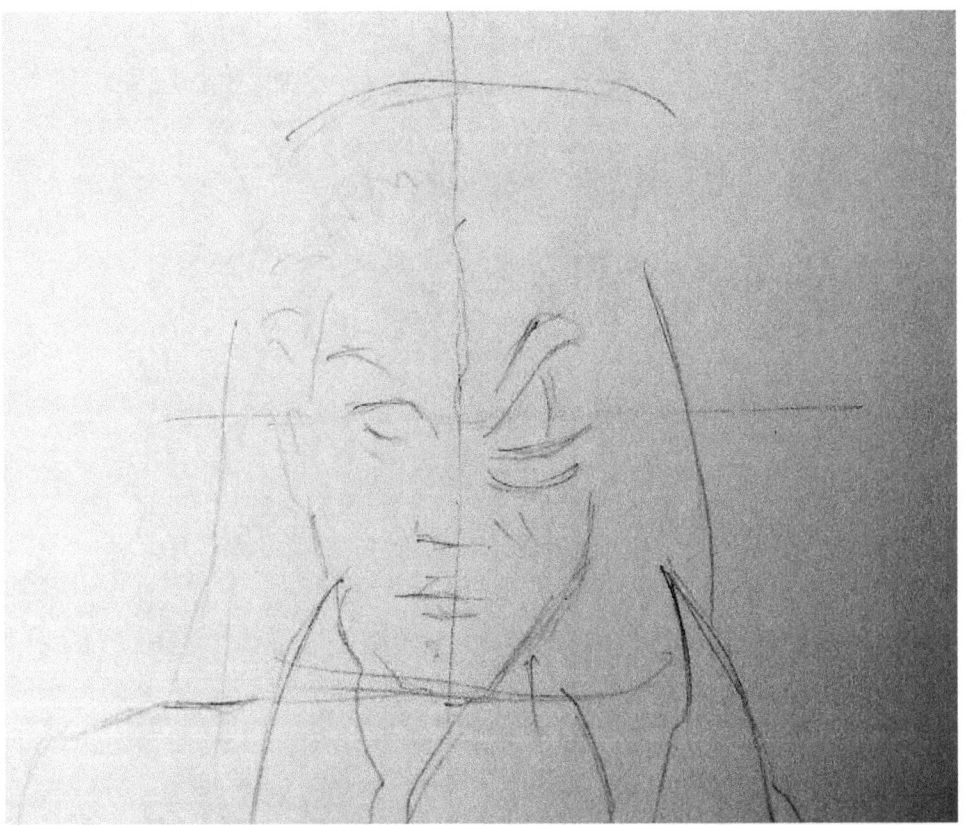

Let's go ahead and block out the areas on the face. Remember that half the face is human, and half of it will be snake, so things may look a little lopsided at this stage. The eye shapes and sizes are going to be different, so there is no symmetry, and this can be difficult.

Just remember to use light lines so that they're easy to erase!

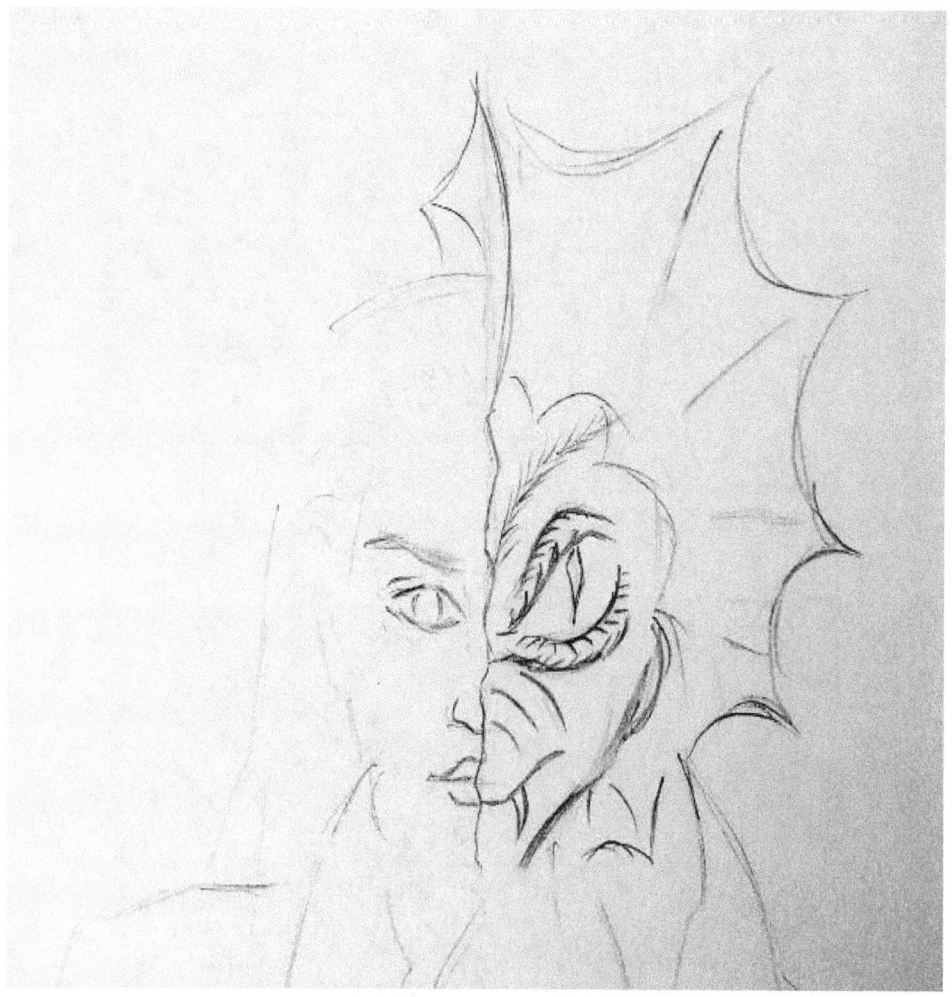

Now we're going to get a few of the details down. The human side will have

one eye, half a nose, and half a mouth. The snake side will have a mouth and

an eye – the mouth of the snake will begin at the bottom lip of the human

side. The snake eye is going to be much bigger than the human eye. Finally, the frills of the snake side are going to be stiff, where the human side will have soft hair.

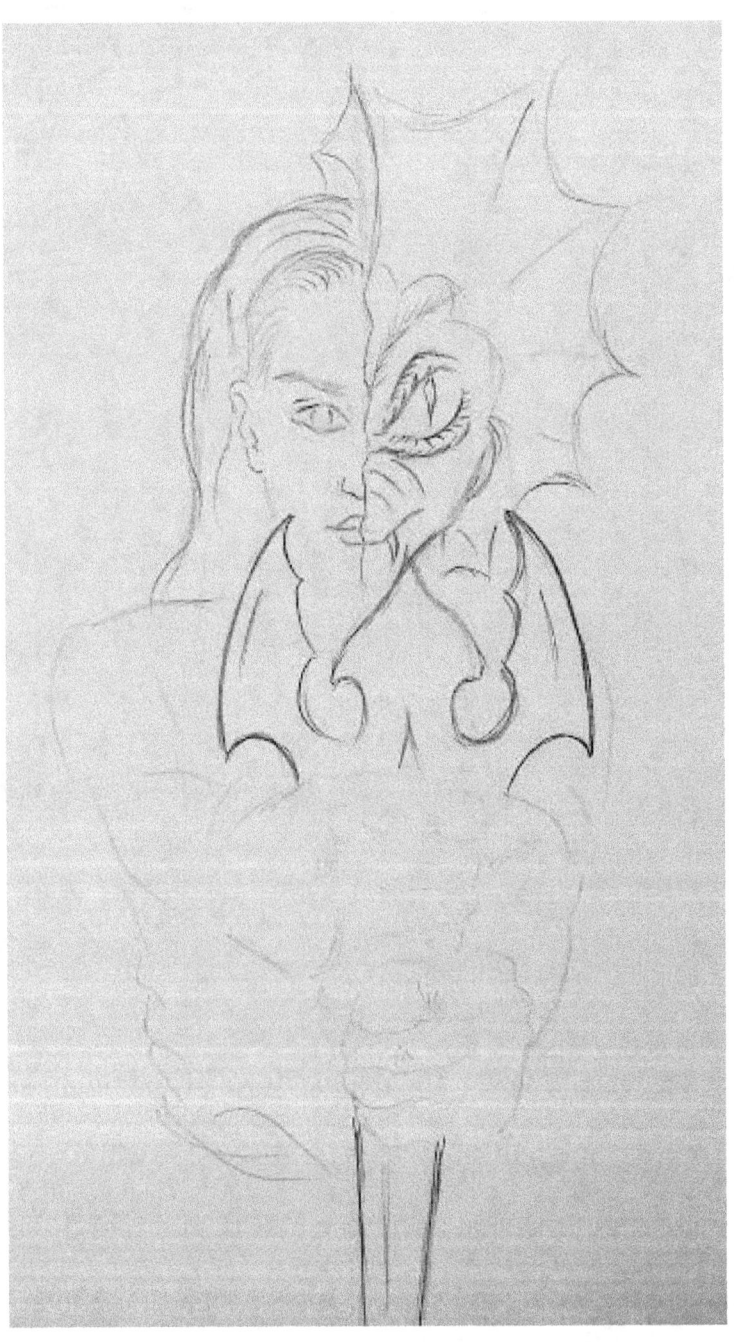

Lightly block in the rest of the body, add some detail to the hair, and work on the weapon. Remember the foreshortening exercise we did with the Horned Girl? This is where it comes into play again.

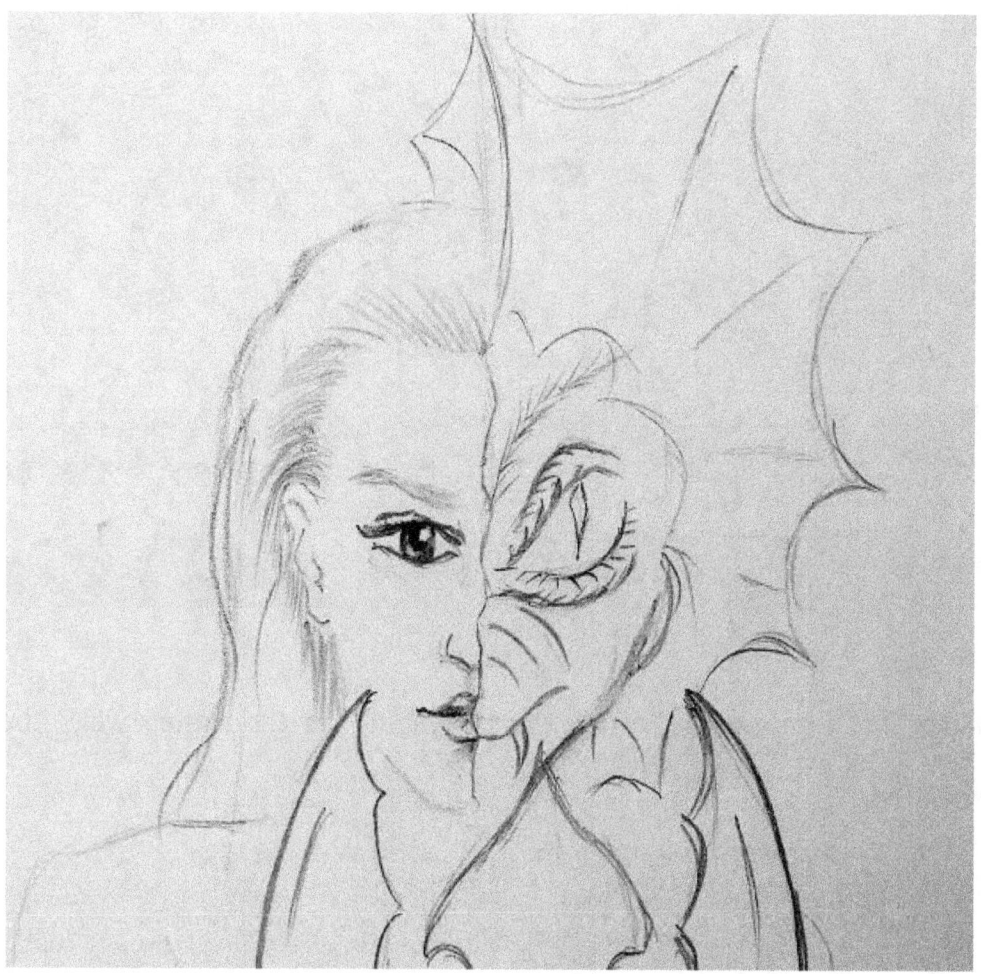

Let's get even more detailed. The human eye is going to have a pupil and an iris, and the human mouth is going to need detail. The hair needs to look light and feathery to contrast the stiffness of the snake side.

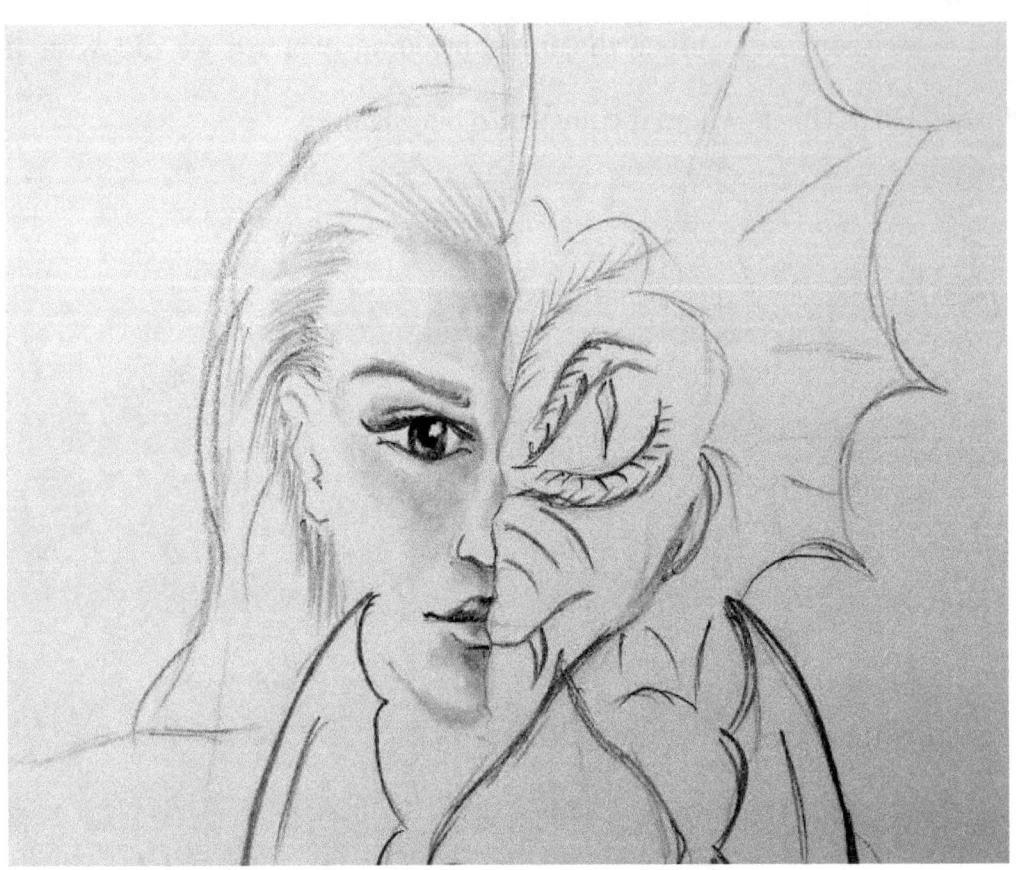

Shade the human side using the smudging method that we've been discussing.

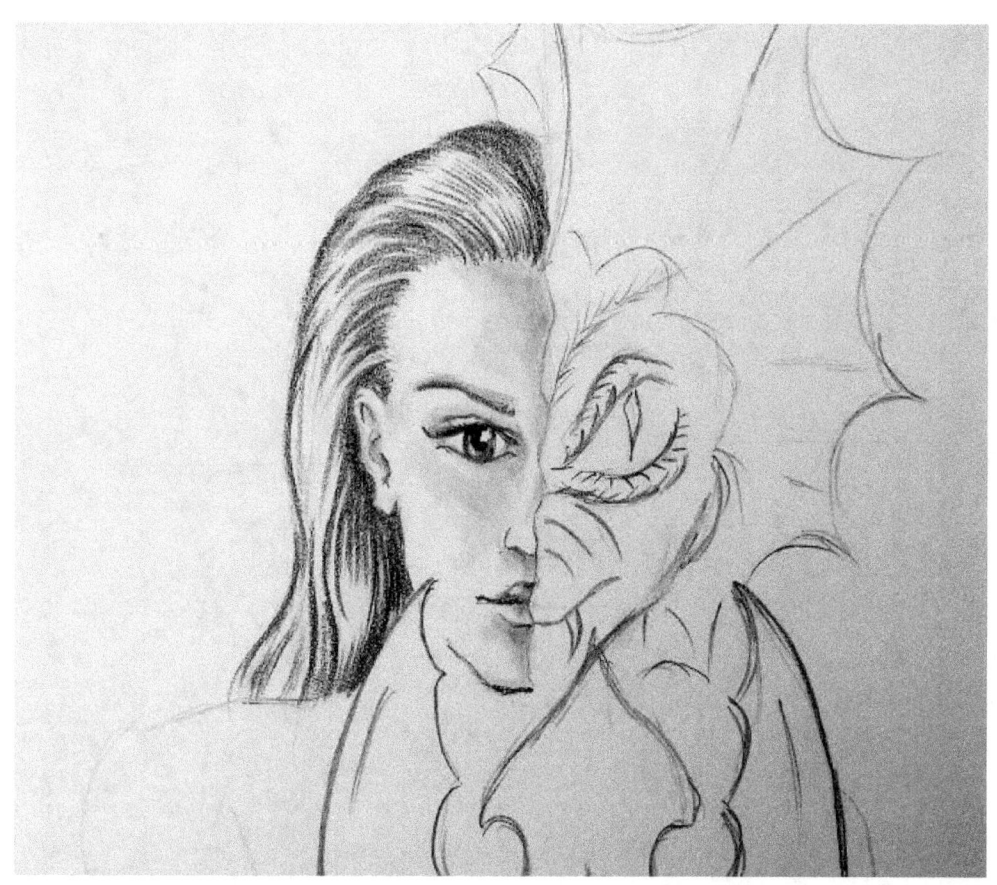

Get a little bit more detailed with the hair, using dark, broad strokes. Make

it look like it is swept back behind her

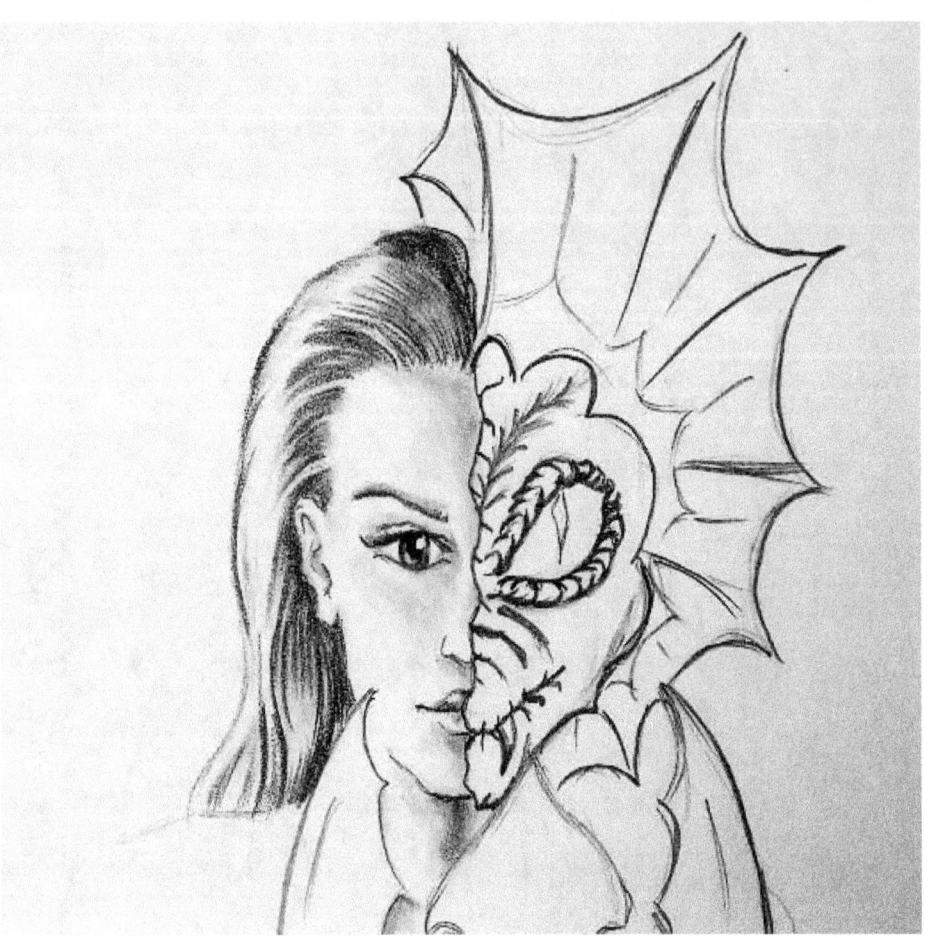

Snakes have scales, and we want to show that. The ridging around the eye and the mouth will help, as will the lines on the snout and above the eye.

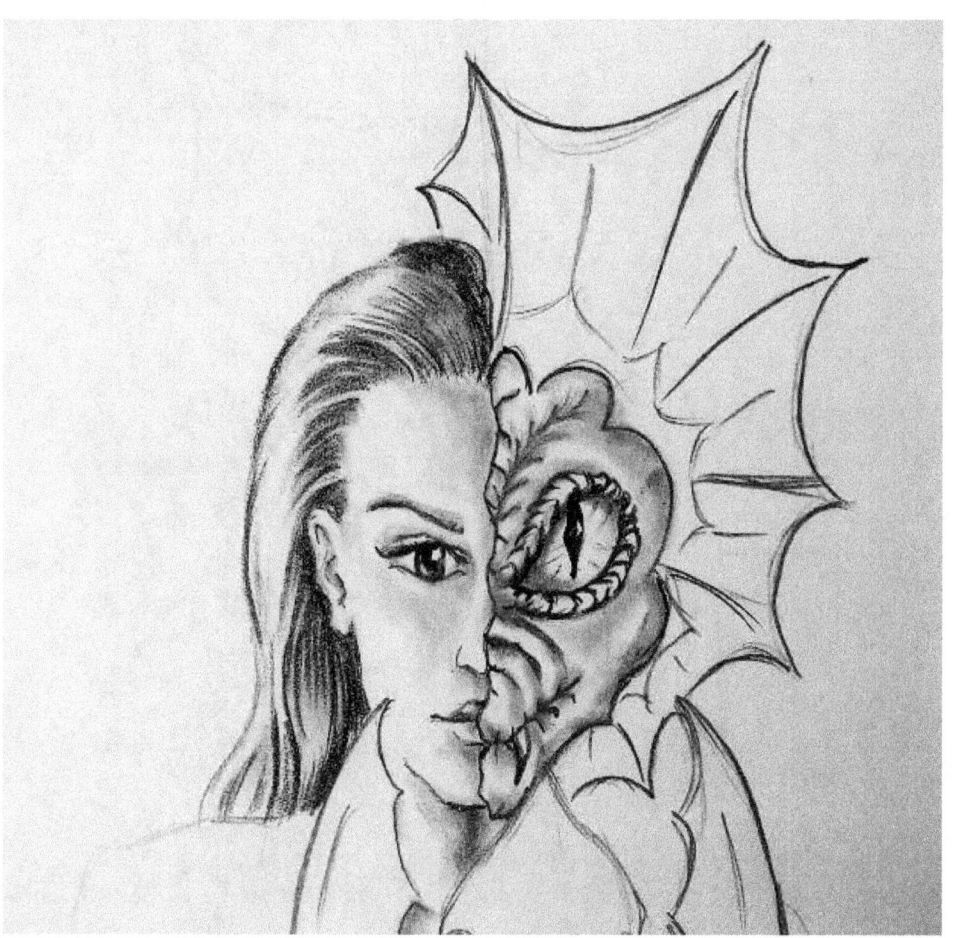

Start to shade the snake side. Notice that it's not as soft as the human side and will require more shading as the shape of the face will be different on this side.

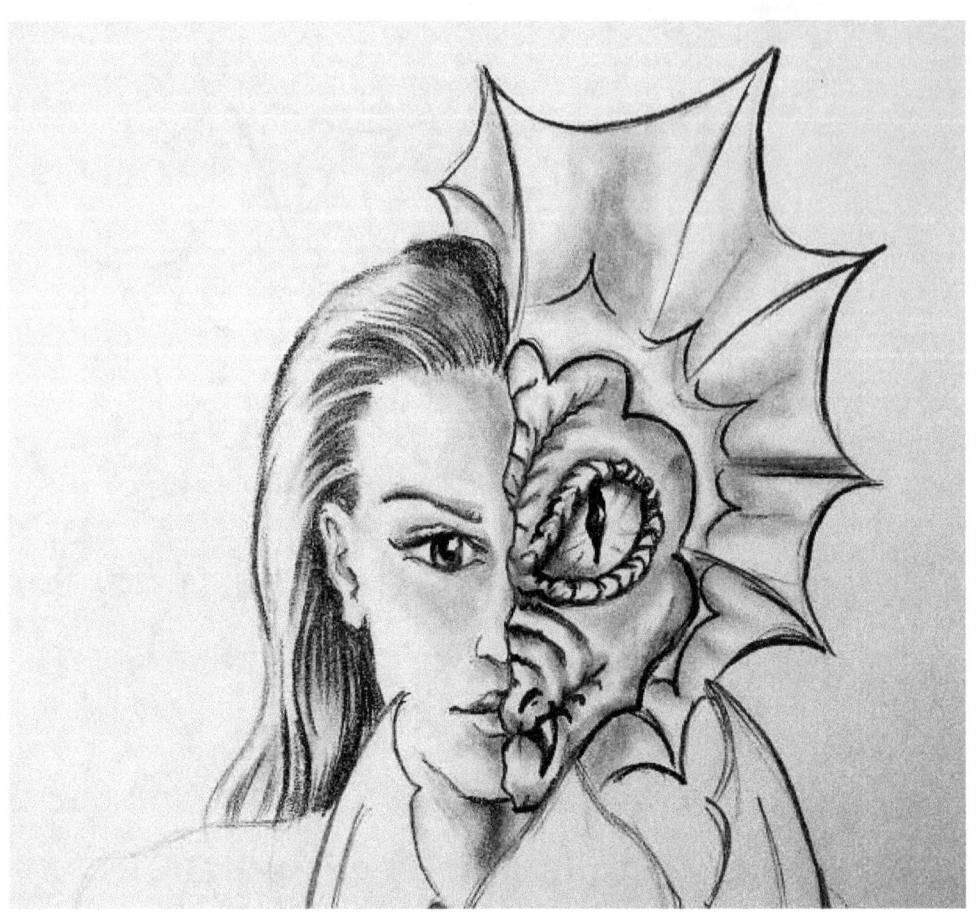

Shade the frills of the snake with the smudging method and darken some of the lines.

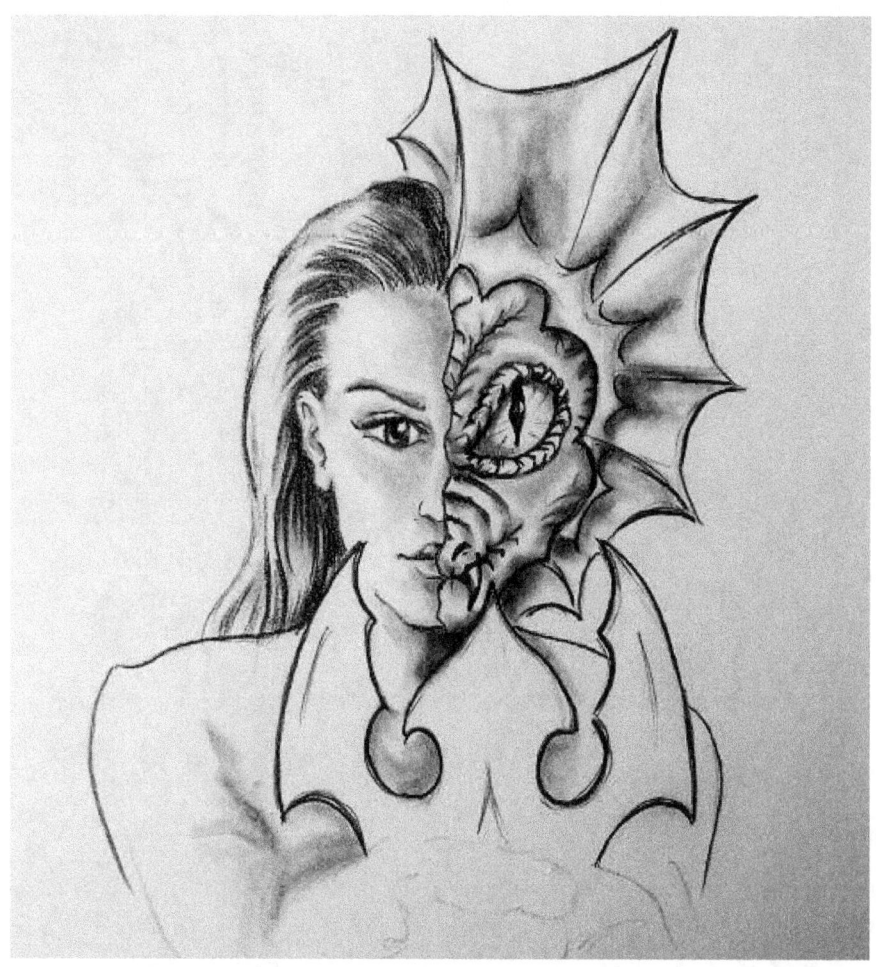

Begin to darken the lines of the body, as well as shading some parts of the

chest, neck, and arm.

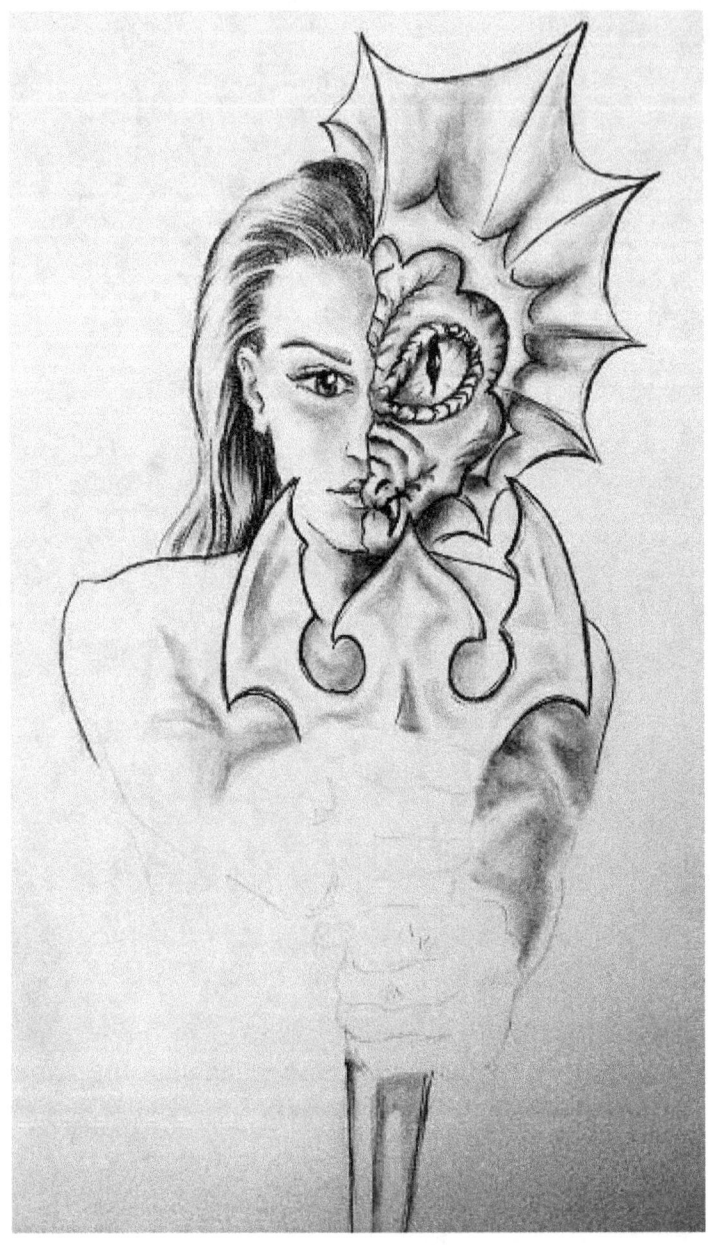

Continue shading the arm, as well as the weapon. Remember the weapon is metal and will have more blocked shapes of shading, rather than a smooth gradient.

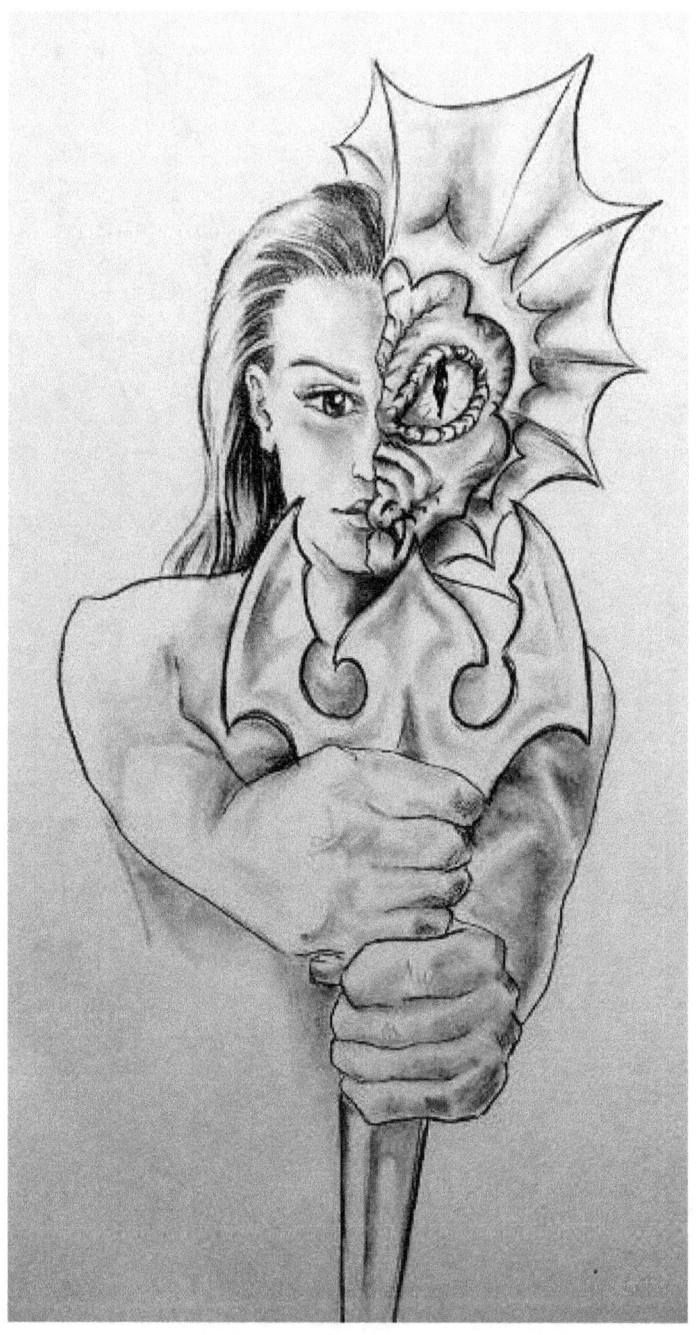

Finish darkening the lines of the hands and shading them.

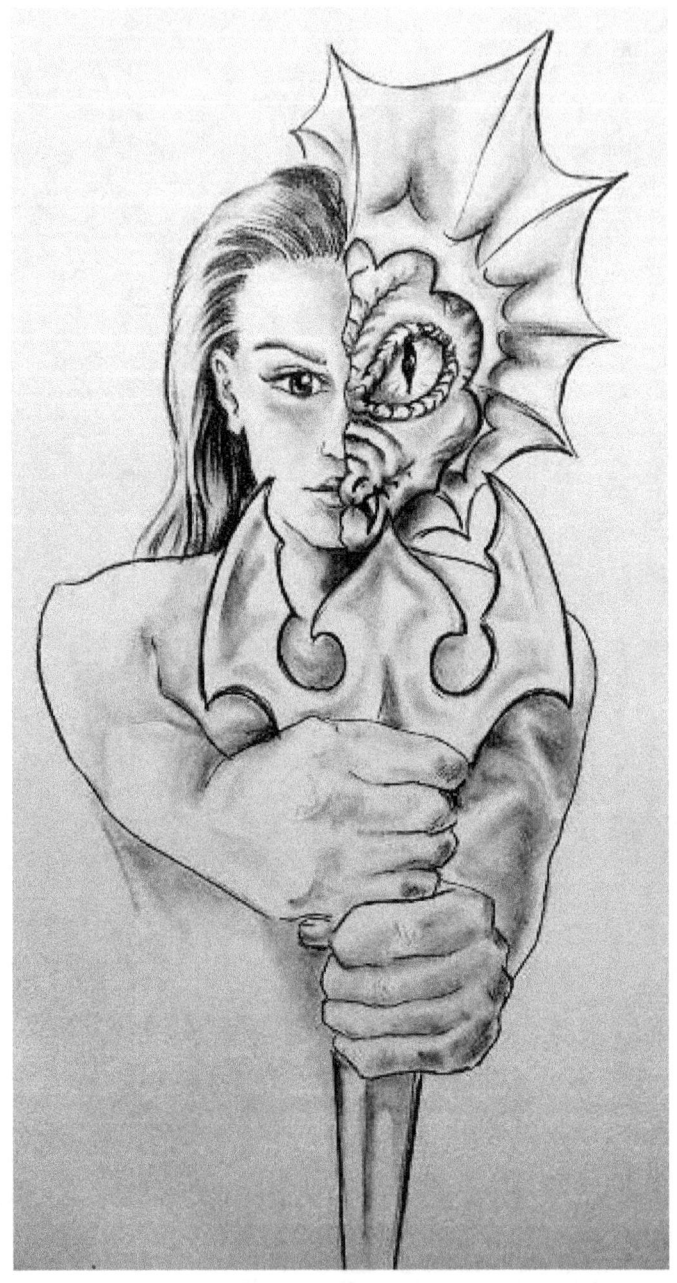

There you have your finished Snake Shifter, ready to slither onto a battlefield or sneak into a castle dungeon late at night. How will you use her in your fantasy world?

Conclusion

Fantasy art is rewarding and fun, and we hope you've had a great time with the tutorials provided. This particular niche of art can be difficult to learn, but it's important to keep trying and keep practicing every day. Whether you draw for a hobby or for a career, this book (and *Fantasy Art Drawing: Step by Step Guide*) has hopefully been a valuable tool in helping you expand your drawing horizons in style, technique, or inspiration.

Foreshortening and smudging are valuable techniques when it comes to working on drawings. For more techniques and drawing tutorials, take a look at *Fantasy Art Drawing: Step by Step Guide* – you can draw dragons, unicorns, and much more.

Fantasy is a great part of our lives, and something to be celebrated. On the other side of the coin, art is something that enriches and empowers us. So, combining the two results in a powerful skill set that can be applied in many different careers, including game design, illustration, and the comic industry. Fantasy art is something to be celebrated and cherished, and we hope that we have enabled you to create things of which you can be proud.

We hope that you have learned something from this book, and we definitely hope it has helped you in your fantastic endeavors!

Thank you!

Thank you for choosing our book, we hope you found it interesting and helpful.

If you liked the book, please give us a favor to write your review.

We would really appreciate this!

If you would like to have a bonus – **FREE BOOK**, please send the screenshot of your review to this e-mail: **kelly.artbooks@gmail.com** and we will send you a **FREE BOOK** in PDF as a **GIFT!****

Hope to see you in our future books and good luck in your drawing experience!

**** in the e-mail subject please mention the name of the book you reviewed and the author.**

Other books by Jong Mac

Dragons Drawing: Step by Step Guide

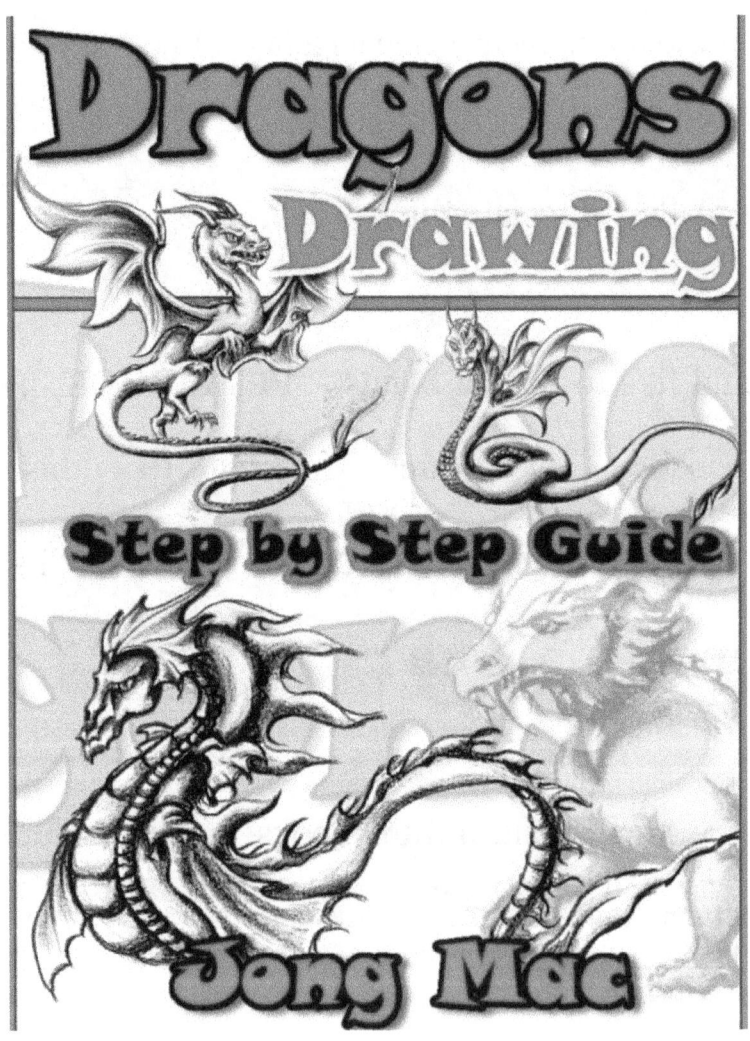

Fantasy Art: Learn How to Draw Amazing Fantasy Girls

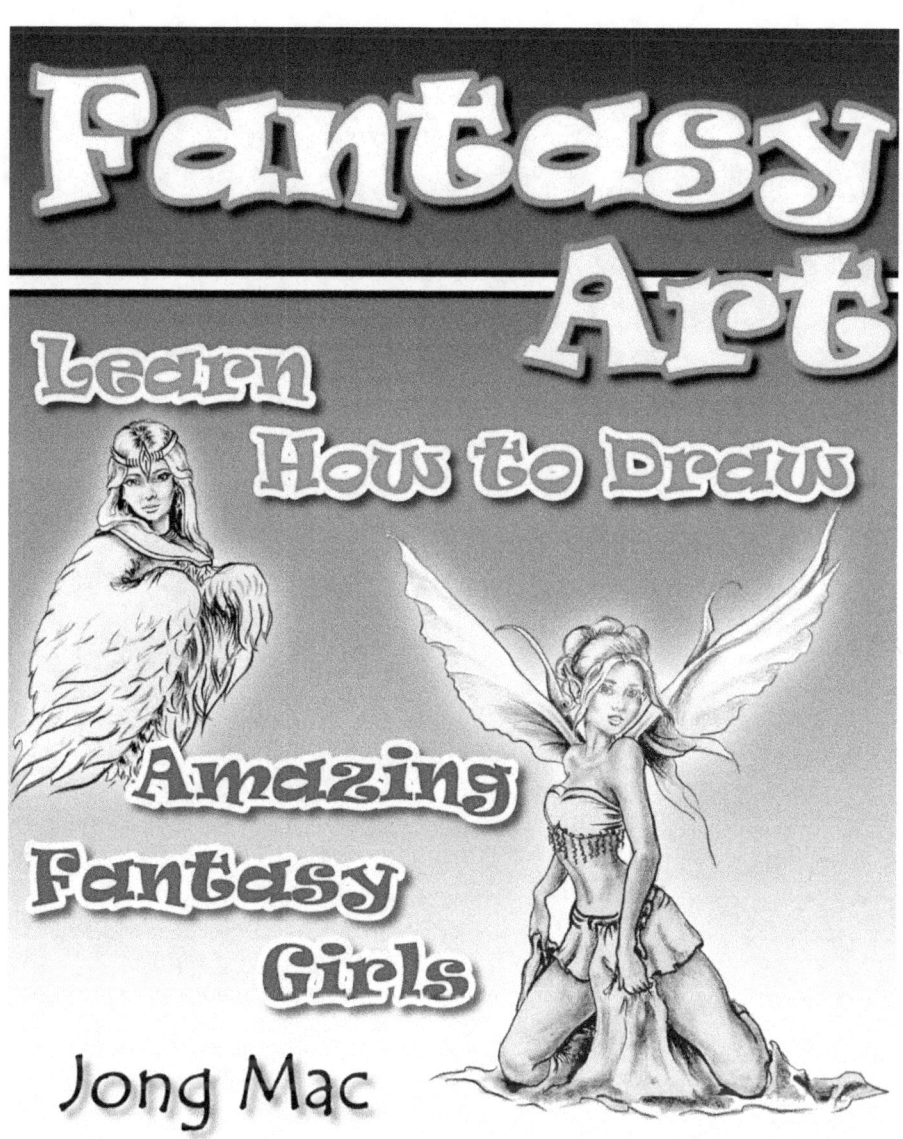

www.ingramcontent.com/pod-product-compliance
Lightning Source LLC
Chambersburg PA
CBHW080715190526
45169CB00006B/2384